" The Reader's Digest
big book of
wit &
wisdom "

" The Reader's Digest
big book of
Wit &
wisdom "

Published by The Reader's Digest Association Limited
London • New York • Sydney • Montreal

CONTENTS

THE WITTY AND THE WISE

Profiles of 12 people renowned for their insightfulness, cleverness and wonderful way with words – plus some of their most memorable quotes.

FEATURES

From weddings and birthdays to insults and last words – eight features for inspiration on life's big occasions, or just for fun.

INTRODUCTION

Welcome to The Reader's Digest Big Book of Wit & Wisdom. One of the most quoted men who ever lived – Winston Churchill – once remarked that 'it is a good thing for an educated man to read books of quotations'. He knew that there is real pleasure in a collection of other people's best thoughts; that genuine insights, well expressed, are priceless gems. This book is a pirate's chest full of jewels of wit and wisdom: leafing through its pages is like plunging your arms deep into that treasure-filled trunk. You never quite know what glittering prize you might find, but you can be pleased that all these finely wrought verbal trinkets, once scattered far and wide, are now within your grasp.

The Reader's Digest Big Book of Wit & Wisdom is a trove containing more than one kind of treasure, though. Some of the quotations are memorable because they are funny, others because they are profound, many because they are both. We hope that you will laugh at the wit, and be moved by the wisdom, but also occasionally smile at the wisdom and be inspired by the wit. After all, the words 'wit' and 'wisdom' are both derived from the same ancient root meaning 'things that are known'. And the one quality that every quotation has in common, whether hilarious or profound, is that below the surface lies a naked truth, something worth knowing.

The more than 3,000 quotations in The Reader's Digest Big Book of Wit & Wisdom are divided into eight thematic chapters, each of which deals with a different aspect of existence such as 'Personal relationships' or 'Vices and virtues'. At every turn of the page, you will find the cream of the cleverest, most delightful remarks ever made on all aspects of our lives and the wider world, such as childhood, marriage, fame, work, courage, friendship, nature, science, art, war and love. As you browse a selection of quotes on any one subject, you may be amazed at the way in which great minds, thinking alike, find such different ways of expressing a similar idea. Then again, there may be times when you are struck by how contradictory the deepest reflections of thoughtful men and women can be even when speaking about the same aspects of life.

Within the chapters
of The Reader's Digest Big Book of Wit
& Wisdom, chock-full of memorable quips, you
will find pages throwing a spotlight on some of the most
prolific and noteworthy quotesmiths of the past two centuries –
political figures such as Martin Luther King, Jnr, and Mahatma Gandhi;
professional jokers such as Mae West, Woody Allen and Groucho Marx; fine
writers with a particular penchant for pithiness such as Oscar Wilde and Dorothy
Parker. These features pick out some of their finest quotes, accompanied by a profile
exploring the reasons why each of these distinguished individuals is so quotable.

Every chapter also contains mini-collections of a different sort – selections of quotations
on life events such as weddings, birthdays, retirement and funerals. These have a practical
purpose: they are there for anyone who has to say a few words on such an occasion, and
would like to enliven their speech with a few firecrackers, or to enrich them with a note of
special solemnity. In addition to these handy features, there are some amusing round-ups
of quotations coined in special circumstances: insulting remarks, political gaffes, last words
and epitaphs. It is amazing to see the amount of effort and creativity that people have invested
into giving their enemies a verbal blasting, or into saying a simple goodbye to the world.

There are many ways to use this book – as a reference (to check, for example, who
made the much misunderstood declaration 'My country, right or wrong' or whether
Greta Garbo really did say 'I want to be alone'), as a source of amusement or
spiritual uplift, as an object lesson in eloquence. However you read it, many
of the things said in The Reader's Digest Big Book of Wit & Wisdom
will stay with you for a long time, and you may find yourself
incorporating certain favourites into your own
conversations. That is all well and good,
but whenever you cite someone else's
brilliant remark, remember the words
of the Canadian novelist Robertson
Davies: 'To be apt in quotation
is a splendid and dangerous
gift,' he said. 'Splendid,
because it ornaments a
man's speech with other
men's jewels; dangerous,
for the same reason.'

KARL MARX

SIGMUND FREUD

MOTHER TERESA

P.G.

RICHARD BRANSON

F. SCOTT FITZGERALD

ERNEST HEMINGWAY

CHARLES DE GAULLE

W. SOMERSET MAUGHAM

PETER USTINOV

MICHELANGELO

EDDIE IZZARD

ALBERT CAMUS

GEORGE BERNARD

ALAN BENNETT

JOAN RIVERS

JONATHAN SWIFT

QUENTIN CRISP

W.H. AUDEN

MUHAMMAD ALI

DOLLY PARTON

JEAN-PAUL SARTRE

GEORGE ORWELL

WALT DISNEY

DOUGLAS ADAMS

JOHN F. KENNEDY

DOROTHY PARKER

ALBERT EINSTEIN

NELSON MANDELA

FRANK ZAPPA

OSCAR WILDE

MARGARET THATCHER

PABLO PICASSO AESOP LEO TOLSTOY ORSON WELLES ISAAC ASIMOV

MARK TWAIN BUDDHA GROUCHO MARX

WODEHOUSE BILL CLINTON VIRGINIA WOOLF

JANE AUSTEN SAMUEL PEPYS

W.C. FIELDS MARILYN MONROE

SHAW MAE WEST BERTRAND RUSSELL

NAPOLEON BONAPARTE

PERSONAL RELATIONSHIPS

Best of friends

> Whenever a friend succeeds, a little something in me dies.
> **Gore Vidal**

I do not believe that friends are necessarily the people you like best, they are merely the people who got there first.

Peter Ustinov

A friend is a second self.

Aristotle

Friendship needs no words. It is solitude delivered from the anguish of loneliness.

Dag Hammarskjöld

A friend may well be reckoned the masterpiece of Nature.

Ralph Waldo Emerson

Friendship is certainly the finest balm for the pangs of disappointed love.

Jane Austen

Often we have no time for our friends but all the time in the world for our enemies.

Leon Uris

It's the friends you can call up at 4am that matter.

Marlene Dietrich

I prefer **acquaintances** to **friends.** They don't expect you to **call** or go to their **children's weddings.**

A.A. Gill

A true friend unbosoms freely, advises justly, assists readily, adventures boldly, defends courageously and continues a friend unchangeably.

William Penn

If we were all given by magic the power to read each other's thoughts, I suppose the first effect would be to dissolve all friendships.

Bertrand Russell

If a man does not make new acquaintance as he advances through life, he will soon find himself left alone. A man, sir, should keep his friendship in constant repair.

Samuel Johnson

Every man should keep a fair-sized cemetery in which to bury the faults of his friends.

Henry Ward Beecher

God's apology for relations.

Hugh Kingsmill

The feeling of friendship is like that of being comfortably filled with roast beef; love, like being enlivened with champagne.

James Boswell

It is one of the blessings of old friends that you can afford to be stupid with them.

Ralph Waldo Emerson

The bird a nest, the spider a web, man friendship.

William Blake

Treat your friends as you do your pictures, and place them in their best light.

Jennie Jerome Churchill

Champagne for my real friends; real pain for my sham friends.

Francis Bacon

Do not remove a fly from your friend's forehead with a hatchet.

Chinese proverb

Your friend is the man who knows all about you and still likes you.

Elbert Hubbard

Be slow to fall into friendship, but when you are in, continue firm and constant.

Socrates

True friends stab you in the front.

Oscar Wilde

Enemies and adversaries

Forgive your enemies, but never forget their names.
John F. Kennedy

Abatement in the hostility of one's enemies must never be thought to signify that they have been won over. It only means that one has ceased to constitute a threat.
Quentin Crisp

You can discover what your enemy fears most by observing the means he uses to frighten you.
Eric Hoffer

It is easier to forgive an enemy than to forgive a friend.
William Blake

You must not fight too often with one enemy, or you will teach him all your art of war.
Napoleon Bonaparte

I hate admitting that my enemies have a point.
Salman Rushdie

A man may learn wisdom even from a foe.
Aristophanes

You shall judge of a man by his foes as well as by his friends.
Joseph Conrad

The best weapon against an enemy is another enemy.
Friedrich Nietzsche

People wish their enemies dead, but I do not. I say give them the gout, give them the stone.
Lady Mary Wortley Montagu

Money can't buy friends, but it can get you a better class of enemy.
Spike Milligan

I choose my friends for their good looks, my acquaintances for their good characters and my enemies for their intellects. A man cannot be too careful in the choice of his enemies.

Oscar Wilde

When my enemies stop hissing, I shall know I'm slipping.

Maria Callas

We often give our enemies the means of our own destruction.

Aesop

Let my enemies devour each other.

Salvador Dalí

It is hard to fight an enemy who has outposts in your head.

Sally Kempton

For a person who cherishes compassion and love, the practice of tolerance is essential; and, for that, an enemy is indispensable.

Dalai Lama

O Lord, make my enemies ridiculous.

Voltaire

You have many enemies that know not why they are so, but, like to village curs, bark when their fellows do.

William Shakespeare

Enemies are so stimulating.

Katharine Hepburn

Ye have heard that it hath been said, Thou shalt love thy neighbour, and hate thine enemy. But I say unto you, Love your enemies, bless them that curse you, do good to them that hate you, and pray for them which despitefully use you, and persecute you ...

The Bible (Gospel of Matthew)

Beware the wrath of a patient adversary.

John C. Calhoun

A wise man gets more use from his enemies than a fool from his friends.

Baltasar Gracian

All in the family

Where does the family start? It starts with a young man falling in love with a girl. No superior alternative has yet been found.

Winston Churchill

Call it a clan, call it a network, call it a tribe, call it a family. Whatever you call it, whoever you are, you need one.

Jane Howard

Far from being the basis of the good society, the family, with its narrow privacy and tawdry secrets, is the source of all our discontents.

Edmund Leach

She knew one of the great family truths, that aunts always help, while moms always think it would be good for you if you did it yourself.

Jane Smiley

Every large family has its angel and its demon.

Joseph Roux

Family quarrels are bitter things. They don't go according to any rules. They're not like aches or wounds; they're more like splits in the skin that won't heal because there's not enough material.

F. Scott Fitzgerald

No matter how many communes anybody invents, the family always creeps back.

Margaret Mead

All happy families are alike; each unhappy family is unhappy in its own way.

Leo Tolstoy

I am the family face;
Flesh perishes, I live on,
Projecting trait and trace
Through time to times anon ...

Thomas Hardy

The human being cannot live too long in the infantile environment, that is, in the bosom of his family, without serious danger to his psychic health.

Carl Jung

Like all the best families, we have our share of eccentricities, of impetuous and wayward youngsters and of family disagreements.

Queen Elizabeth II

Family … the home of all social evil, a charitable institution for comfortable women, an anchorage for house-fathers and a hell for children.

August Strindberg

Family jokes, though rightly cursed by strangers, are the bond that keeps most families alive.

Stella Benson

A brother is a friend given by Nature.

Gabriel Marie Legouvé

The awe and dread with which the untutored savage contemplates his mother-in-law are amongst the most familiar facts of anthropology.

James G. Frazer

Every man sees in his relatives, and especially in his cousins, a series of grotesque caricatures of himself.

H.L. Mencken

Without a family, man, alone in the world, trembles with the cold.

André Maurois

To the family – that dear octopus from whose tentacles we never quite escape nor, in our inmost hearts, ever quite wish to.

Dodie Smith

A family's photograph album is generally about the extended family – and, often, is all that remains of it.

Susan Sontag

As to the family, I have never understood why it should be an ideal at all. A group of closely related persons, living under one roof; it is a convenience, often a necessity, sometimes a pleasure, sometimes the reverse; but who first exalted it as admirable?

Rose Macaulay

The family is the homeland of the heart.

Giuseppe Mazzini

There is no such thing as 'fun for the whole family'.
Jerry Seinfeld

Mothers and fathers

I have only two rules for my newly born daughter. She will dress well; she will never have sex.

John Malkovich

Parents should conduct their arguments in quiet, respectful tones, but in a foreign language. You'd be surprised what an inducement that is to the education of children.

Judith Martin

No one but doctors and mothers know what it means to have interruptions.

Karl A. Menninger

Don't parents get blamed too much for over-influencing their children, when the blame should mostly lie on the children for not kicking more strenuously against their influence?

C.E. Montague

I could not point to any need in childhood as strong as that for a father's protection.

Sigmund Freud

Better to play 15 minutes enjoyably and then say, 'Now I'm going to read my paper' than to spend all day at the zoo crossly.

Dr Benjamin Spock

A mother never realises that her children are no longer children.

Holbrook Jackson

No man can possibly know what life means, what the world means, what anything means, until he has a child and loves it.

Lafcadio Hearn

Level with your child by being honest. Nobody spots a phony quicker than a child.

Mary MacCracken

Having one child makes you a parent; having two you are a referee.

David Frost

Grown-ups never understand anything for themselves, and it is tiresome for children to be always and forever explaining things to them.

Antoine de Saint-Exupéry

It doesn't matter who my father was; it matters who I remember he was.

Anne Sexton

As is the mother, so is her daughter.

The Bible (Ezekiel)

If you must hold yourself up to your children as an object lesson (which is not at all necessary), hold yourself up as a warning and not as an example.

George Bernard Shaw

Whatever else is unsure in this stinking dunghill of a world a mother's love is not.

James Joyce

Never help a child with a task at which he feels he can succeed.

Maria Montessori

If you bungle raising your children, I don't think whatever else you do matters very much.

Jackie Kennedy Onassis

There are two things in life for which we are never truly prepared: twins.

Josh Billings

Motherhood is like sex and death; you can't imagine it until you do it. It's completely overwhelming, all-else obliterating passion for a little blob!

Juliet Stevenson

There is no more sombre enemy of good art than the pram in the hall.

Cyril Connolly

In our society ... mothers go on getting blamed until they're 80, but shouldn't take it personally.

Katharine Whitehorn

Father and son are natural enemies and each is happier and more secure in keeping it that way.

John Steinbeck

I have four sons and three stepsons. I have learnt what it is like to step on Lego with bare feet.

Fay Weldon

Quotations
for **weddings**

The happiest day of your life – or potentially the most terrifying if you have to stand up to say a few words about the bride, groom or even mother-in-law. For inspiration, and a little help with that speech, here are some thoughtful insights on wedded bliss.

Place me like a seal over your heart, like a seal on your arm; for love is as strong as death, its jealousy unyielding as the grave. It burns like blazing fire, like a mighty flame. Many waters cannot quench love; rivers cannot wash it away. If one were to give all the wealth of his house for love, it would be utterly scorned.

The Bible (Song of Solomon)

Wedlock is the deep, deep peace of the double bed after the hurly-burly of the chaise longue.

Mrs Patrick Campbell

Intimacy is what makes a marriage, not a ceremony, not a piece of paper from the state.

Kathleen Norris

What greater thing is there for two human souls, than to feel that they are joined for life – to strengthen each other in all labour, to rest on each other in all sorrow, to minister to each other in all pain, to be one with each other in silent unspeakable memories at the moment of the last parting?

George Eliot

Marriage is not a noun; it's a verb. It isn't something you get. It's something you do. It's the way you love your partner every day.

Barbara De Angelis

A great marriage is not when the 'perfect couple' comes together. It is when an imperfect couple learns to enjoy their differences.

Dave Meurer

*Let all thy joys be as the month of May,
And all thy days be as a marriage day.*

Francis Quarles

JUST MARRIED!

A single man has not nearly the value he would have in a state of union. He is an incomplete animal. He resembles the odd half of a pair of scissors.

Benjamin Franklin

Matrimony: friendship under difficult circumstances.

Rose Scott

Love one another and you will be happy. It's as simple and as difficult as that.

Michael Leunig

Who, being loved, is poor?

Oscar Wilde

Let there be spaces in your togetherness and let the winds of the heavens dance between you. Love one another but make not a bond of love: let it rather be a moving sea between the shores of your souls. Fill each other's cup, but drink not from one cup.

Kahlil Gibran

There is in marriage an energy and an impulse of joy that lasts as long as life and that survives all sorts of suffering and distress and weariness. The triumph of marriage over all its antagonists is almost inexplicable.

James Douglas

Two human loves make one divine.

Elizabeth Barrett Browning

Come live with me and be my love,
And we will some new pleasures prove
Of golden sands and crystal brooks,
With silken lines and silver hooks.

John Donne

A successful marriage requires falling in love many times, always with the same person.

Mignon McLaughlin

God, the best maker of all marriages, Combine your hearts into one.

William Shakespeare

A fine
romance

Men seldom make passes at girls who wear glasses.
Dorothy Parker

The mark of a true crush is that you fall in love first and grope for reasons afterward.

Shana Alexander

In real love you want the other person's good. In romantic love you want the other person.

Margaret Anderson

Love is a fan club with only two fans.

Adrian Henri

Always carry a book on a date so that when you get bored you can slip into the Ladies for a read.

Sharon Stone

Passion is the quickest to develop, and the quickest to fade. Intimacy develops more slowly, and commitment more gradually still.

Robert Sternberg

Nothing spoils a romance so much as a sense of humour in the woman – or the want of it in the man.

Oscar Wilde

If grass can grow through cement, love can find you at every time in your life.

Cher

Love is universal migraine,
A bright stain on the vision
Blotting out reason.

Robert Graves

Love is a fire. But whether it is going to warm your hearth or burn down your house, you can never tell.

Joan Crawford

When you love a man, he becomes more than a body. His physical limbs expand, and his outline recedes, vanishes. He is rich and sweet and right. He is part of the world, the atmosphere, the blue sky and the blue water.

Gwendolyn Brooks

To fall in love is to create a religion that has a fallible god.

Jorge Luis Borges

I was born when you kissed me. I died when you left me.
I lived a few weeks while you loved me.

Humphrey Bogart

I wonder what fool it was that first invented kissing.

Jonathan Swift

A kiss is a lovely trick designed by nature to stop speech
when words become superfluous.

Ingrid Bergman

There is a place you can touch a woman that will drive her
crazy. Her heart.

Melanie Griffith

The sound of a kiss is not so loud as that of a cannon,
but its echo lasts a great deal longer.

Oliver Wendell Holmes

In love, one and one are one.

Jean-Paul Sartre

A man is already halfway in love with any woman
who listens to him.

Brendan Francis

Love is an act of endless forgiveness,
a tender look which becomes a habit.
Peter Ustinov

Love is a perky elf dancing
a merry little jig and then
suddenly he turns on
you with a miniature
machine gun.
Matt Groening

One is very crazy
when in love.
Sigmund Freud

Once in his life, every
man is entitled to fall
madly in love with a
gorgeous redhead.
Lucille Ball

All you need is love

I here and now, finally and forever, give up knowing anything about love, or wanting to know. I believe it doesn't exist, save as a word. It's a sort of wailing phoenix that is really the wind in the trees.

D.H. Lawrence

I don't want to live. I want to love first, and live incidentally.

Zelda Fitzgerald

> Love is the triumph of imagination over intelligence.
>
> **H.L. Mencken**

You will find as you look back upon your life that the moments when you have truly lived are the moments when you have done things in the spirit of love.

Henry Drummond

Love is an exploding cigar we willingly smoke.

Lynda Barry

Love doesn't just sit there, like a stone; it has to be made, like bread, remade all the time, made new.

Ursula K. Le Guin

The first duty of love is to listen.

Paul Tillich

Looking back, I have this to regret, that too often when I loved, I did not say so.

David Grayson

Love him and let him love you. Do you think anything else under heaven really matters?

James Baldwin

You never lose by loving. You always lose by holding back.

Barbara De Angelis

Among those whom I like or admire, I can find no common denominator, but among those whom I love, I can: all of them make me laugh.

W.H. Auden

There is love, of course. And then there's life, its enemy.

Jean Anouilh

People are unreasonable, illogical, and self-centred. Love them anyway.

Mother Teresa

Love is staying up all night with a sick child – or a healthy adult.

David Frost

Love builds bridges where there are none.

R.H. Delaney

I have a very strong feeling that the opposite of love is not hate – it's apathy. It's not giving a damn.

Leo Buscaglia

The heart of another is a dark forest, always, no matter how close it has been to one's own.

Willa Cather

It is not love that is blind, but jealousy.

Lawrence Durrell

Love is patient, love is kind. It does not envy, it does not boast, it is not proud. It is not rude, it is not self-seeking, it is not easily angered, it keeps no record of wrongs. Love does not delight in evil but rejoices with the truth. It always protects, always trusts, always hopes, always perseveres. Love never fails.

The Bible (I Corinthians)

Love is an irresistible desire to be irresistibly desired.

Robert Frost

No, there's nothing half so sweet in life As love's young dream.

Thomas Moore

'Tis better to have loved and lost than never to have loved at all.

Alfred, Lord Tennyson

Love is like a cigar. If it goes out, you can light it again – but it never tastes quite the same.

Lord Wavell

Marriage and matrimony

> In a two-car family, the wife always has the smaller car.
>
> **Ruth Rendell**

My advice to you is get married: if you find a good wife you'll be happy; if not, you'll become a philosopher.

Socrates

It's not a good idea to put your wife into a novel; not your latest wife anyway.

Norman Mailer

I used to believe that marriage would diminish me, reduce my options. That you had to be someone less to live with someone else when, of course, you have to be someone more.

Candice Bergen

A man would often be the lover of his wife if he were married to someone else.

Elinor Glyn

It's impossible to live at peace with anyone you love. You can only live at peace with those to whom you are indifferent.

Martin Boyd

I feel sure that no girl would go to the altar if she knew all.

Queen Victoria

In every marriage more than a week old, there are grounds for divorce. The trick is to find, and continue to find, grounds for marriage.

Robert Anderson

My wife and I were happy for 20 years. Then we met.

Rodney Dangerfield

It seemed to me that the desire to get married – which, I regret to say, I believe is basic and primal in women – is followed almost immediately by an equally basic and primal urge – which is to be single again.

Nora Ephron

The married are those who have taken the terrible risk of intimacy and, having taken it, know life without intimacy to be impossible.

Carolyn G. Heilbrun

The majority of husbands remind me of an orangutan trying to play the violin.

Honoré de Balzac

A happy marriage is the world's best bargain.

O.A. Battista

I married beneath me, all women do.

Nancy Astor

An **archaeologist** is the best husband a **woman** can have; the older she gets the **more interested** he is in her.

Agatha Christie

There is more to marriage than four bare legs under a blanket.

Robertson Davies

The best way to get husbands to do something is to suggest that they are too old to do it.

Shirley MacLaine

Strange to say what delight we married people have to see these poor fools decoyed into our condition.

Samuel Pepys

Most wives think of their husbands as bumbling braggarts with whom they happen to be in love.

Jackie Gleason

Chumps always make the best husbands. When you marry, Sally, grab a chump.

P.G. Wodehouse

Keep your eyes wide open before marriage, half shut afterwards.

Benjamin Franklin

Never feel remorse for what you've thought about your wife, for she's thought much worse things about you.

Jean Rostand

I believe in the institution of marriage, and I intend to keep trying till I get it right.

Richard Pryor

Sex and seduction

In my sex fantasy, nobody ever loves me for my mind.
Nora Ephron

Intimate relationships cannot substitute for a life plan. But to have any meaning or viability at all, a life plan must include intimate relationships.

Harriet Lerner

Pursuit and seduction are the essence of sexuality. It's part of the sizzle.

Camille Paglia

The only unnatural sex act is that which you cannot perform.

Alfred Kinsey

If all the girls who attended the Yale prom were laid end to end, I wouldn't be at all surprised.

Dorothy Parker

I often think that a slightly exposed shoulder emerging from a long satin nightgown packs more sex than two naked bodies in bed.

Bette Davis

Whatever else can be said about sex, it cannot be called a dignified performance.

Helen Lawrenson

Sex alleviates tension. Love causes it.

Woody Allen

Women need a reason to have sex. Men just need a place.
Billy Crystal

A woman making up her lips is like a soldier preparing his machine gun.

Sigmund Freud

There is nothing like early promiscuous sex for dispelling life's bright mysterious expectations.

Iris Murdoch

Chastity: the most unnatural of the sexual perversions.

Aldous Huxley

In America sex is an obsession, in other parts of the world it is a fact.

Marlene Dietrich

Among men, sex sometimes results in intimacy; among women, intimacy sometimes results in sex.

Barbara Cartland

Do not adultery commit;
Advantage rarely comes of it.

Arthur Hugh Clough

Adultery is the application of democracy to love.

H.L. Mencken

Men who are too good looking are never good in bed because they never had to be.

Cindy Chupack

Men lose more conquests by their own awkwardness than by any virtue in the woman.

Ninon de Lenclos

I'm always looking for meaningful one-night stands.

Dudley Moore

Sex without love is an empty experience, but as empty experiences go it's a pretty good one.

Woody Allen

Sex is one of the most wholesome, beautiful and natural experiences that money can buy.

Steve Martin

Pornography is rather like trying to find out about a Beethoven symphony by having somebody tell you about it and perhaps hum a few bars.

Robertson Davies

Sex is a momentary itch; love never lets you go.

Kingsley Amis

Sex has never been an obsession with me. It's just like eating a bag of crisps. Quite nice, but nothing marvellous.

Boy George

Brevity is the soul of lingerie.

Dorothy Parker

Sex: the thing that takes up the least amount of time and causes the most amount of trouble.

John Barrymore

Mae West

HIGH PRIESTESS OF SAUCE

The feisty New Yorker talked about sex in a way that was funny, vulgar and unashamed. This made Mae West popular with her audiences, but branded her as an enemy of censors and self-appointed moral guardians. In 1926 she spent a week in jail for having written and produced a play called *Sex*, which was judged to be 'corrupting the morals of youth'. The publicity that her imprisonment brought was, inevitably, a huge boost to her career.

West was in some ways an unlikely sex symbol, since she was almost 40 when she made her first film. Her famously curvaceous figure was never on show unless moulded and buttressed by elaborate corsetry. It was her wit and her personality that made her sexy – and she wrote all her best lines herself. 'Is that a gun in your pocket or are you just glad to see me' was one of hers; 'I've been things and I've seen places' was another.

The sexual emancipation of the 1960s rendered West's risqué humour obsolete, but some of her sayings became proverbial expressions. Her contention that 'too much of a good thing can be wonderful' is often cited, as is the alluring (but misquoted) invitation to 'come up and see me some time'. What she actually said, to Cary Grant in the 1933 film *She Done Him Wrong*, was 'Why don't you come up some time and see me?'

✳

Between two evils, I always pick the one I never tried before.

✳

I generally avoid temptation unless I can't resist it.

✳

When I'm good I'm very, very good,
but when I'm bad I'm better.

✳

I only like two kinds of men: domestic and foreign.

✳

A woman in love can't be reasonable –
or she probably wouldn't be in love.

✳

A man's kiss is his signature.

✳

Personality is the most important thing to an actress's
success. Personality is the glitter that sends your
little gleam across the footlights and the orchestra pit
into that big black space where the audience is.

✳

If I asked for a cup of coffee,
someone would search for the double meaning.

✳

I used to be Snow White … but I drifted.

Men will be men

Can you imagine a world without men? No crime and lots of happy fat women.

Nicole Hollander

Every modern male has, lying at the bottom of his psyche, a large, primitive being covered with hair down to his feet. Making contact with this Wild Man is the step the 80s man or the 90s man has yet to take.

Robert Bly

No nice men are good at getting taxis.

Katharine Whitehorn

There is, of course, no reason for the existence of the male sex except that sometimes one needs help with moving the piano.

Rebecca West

Whereas nature turns girls into women, society has to make boys into men.

Anthony Stevens

Men are all the same. They always think that something they are going to get is better than what they have got.

John Oliver Hobbes

Someone has to stand up for wimps.

Barbara Ehrenreich

The male sex still constitute in many ways the most obstinate vested interest one can find.

Lord Longford

If you would understand men, study women.

French proverb

A man who has nothing to do with women is always incomplete.

Cyril Connolly

Don't accept rides from strange men, and remember that all men are strange.

Robin Morgan

Windjacket in **Emu** SCOTCH DOUBLE KNITTING

6ᴰ

I wonder why men can get serious at all. They have this delicate long thing hanging outside their bodies, which goes up and down by its own will … if I were a man I would always be laughing at myself.

Yoko Ono

If the world were a logical place, men would ride sidesaddle.

Rita Mae Brown

I'm a lesbian trapped in a man's body.

Eddie Izzard

Whether he admits it or not, a man has been brought up to look at money as a sign of his virility, a symbol of his power, a bigger phallic symbol than a Porsche.

Victoria Billings

Not only is it harder to be a man, it is harder to become one.

Arianna Huffington

The average man is more interested in a woman who is interested in him than in a woman – any woman – with beautiful legs.

Marlene Dietrich

The male is a domestic animal which, if treated with firmness, can be trained to do most things.

Jilly Cooper

It's not the men in my life that counts – it's the life in my men.

Mae West

One of the things being in politics has taught me is that men are not a reasoned or reasonable sex.

Margaret Thatcher

Sigh no more, ladies, sigh no more,
Men were deceivers ever,
One foot in sea and one on shore,
To one thing constant never.

William Shakespeare

Men should be like Kleenex – soft, strong and disposable.
Cher

There was **never** a great man who had not a **great mother**.

Olive Schreiner

I love the male body. It's better designed than the male mind.
Andrea Newman

The **female** of the **species**

The female of the species is more deadly than the male.
Rudyard Kipling

It can be less painful for a woman not to hear the strange dissatisfied voice stirring within her.

Betty Friedan

I am not a do-gooder. I am a revolutionary. A revolutionary woman.

Jane Fonda

When once a woman has given you her heart, you can never get rid of the rest of her body.

John Vanbrugh

I think the key is for women not to set any limits.

Martina Navratilova

People think at the end of the day that a man is the only answer. Actually a job is better for me.

Diana, Princess of Wales

Once a man is on hand, a woman tends to stop believing in her own beliefs.

Colette Dowling

Women who seek to be **equal** **with men** lack ambition.

Timothy Leary

A woman is like a tea bag – you never know how strong she is until she gets in hot water.

Eleanor Roosevelt

I'd like to get to the point where we can be just as mediocre as a man.

Juanita Kreps

I have a brain and a uterus, and I use them both.

Patricia Schroeder

The great question that has never been answered, and which I have not yet been able to answer, despite my 30 years of research into the feminine soul, is 'What does a woman want?'

Sigmund Freud

So few grown women like their lives.

Katharine Graham

A woman must have money and a room of her own if she is to write fiction.

Virginia Woolf

The thing women have yet to learn is nobody gives you power. You just take it.

Roseanne Barr

Women are like elephants to me: nice to look at, but I wouldn't want to own one.

W.C. Fields

It's the women who make decisions. Women are strong, women are the doers, that's the way it is.

Eugenie Clark

A girl can wait for the right man to come along, but in the meantime that still doesn't mean she can't have a wonderful time with all the wrong ones.

Cher

Feminism is an entire world view, not just a laundry list of 'women's issues'.

Charlotte Bunch

Women should be obscene and not heard.

Groucho Marx

Some of us are becoming the men we wanted to marry.

Gloria Steinem

I am a woman meant for a man, but I never found a man who could compete.

Bette Davis

You don't know a woman until you have had a letter from her.

Ada Leverson

If you want anything said, ask a man. If you want something done, ask a woman.

Margaret Thatcher

> It's the good girls who keep diaries; the bad girls never have the time.
>
> **Tallulah Bankhead**

The **battle** of the **sexes**

In societies where men are truly confident of their own worth, women are not merely tolerated but valued.

Aung San Suu Kyi

Friendship can only exist between persons with similar interests and points of view. Man and woman by the conventions of society are born with different interests and different points of view.

August Strindberg

Women have very little idea of how much men hate them.

Germaine Greer

Women deprived of the company of men pine, men deprived of the company of women become stupid.

Anton Chekhov

There is more difference within the sexes than between them.

Ivy Compton-Burnett

Behind every famous man is a woman who says there is a woman behind every famous man.

Hal Roach

Whatever women do they must do twice as well as men to be thought half as good. Luckily this is not difficult.

Charlotte Whitton

Nagging is the repetition of unpalatable truths.

Edith Summerskill

There are times when even a dedicated feminist needs a chauvinist to lean on.

Clive Cussler

Women might be able to fake orgasms, but men can fake a whole relationship.

Sharon Stone

There is no reciprocity. Men love women, women love children, children love hamsters.

Alice Thomas Ellis

Nobody will ever win the battle of the sexes. There's too much fraternising with the enemy.

Henry Kissinger

Men want the same thing from their underwear that they want from women: a little bit of support, and a little bit of freedom.

Jerry Seinfeld

A man who correctly guesses a woman's age may be smart, but he's not very bright.

Lucille Ball

The first problem for all of us, men and women, is not to learn but to unlearn.

Gloria Steinem

A man's brain has a more difficult time shifting from thinking to feeling than a woman's brain does.

Barbara De Angelis

> A woman without a man is like a fish without a bicycle.
> **Gloria Steinem**

The only time a woman really succeeds in changing a man is when he's a baby.

Natalie Wood

It is better to be unfaithful than faithful without wanting to be.

Brigitte Bardot

Men kick friendship round like a football and it doesn't seem to crack. Women treat it like glass and it goes to pieces.

Anon

Women want mediocre men, and men are working hard to become as mediocre as possible.

Margaret Mead

A man can sleep around, no questions asked, but if a woman makes 19 or 20 mistakes she's a tramp.

Joan Rivers

A man never knows how to say good-bye; a woman never knows when to say it.

Helen Rowland

Most women set out to try to change a man, and when they have changed him they do not like him.

Marlene Dietrich

Society at large

> Society needs to condemn a little more and understand a little less.
> **John Major**

Our society is run by insane people for insane objectives. I think we're being run by maniacs for maniacal ends and I think I'm liable to be put away as insane for expressing that. That's what's insane about it.

John Lennon

The spirit of truth and the spirit of freedom – these are the pillars of society.

Henrik Ibsen

All the world over, I will back the masses against the classes.

William Gladstone

No man is an island, entire of itself. Each is a piece of the continent, a part of the main.

John Donne

Every man thinks himself the social superior of every other. The truth is that one man is as good as another, if he is as good; and none of us any better than we should be.

Miles Franklin

Civilisation is a movement, not a condition; a voyage and not a harbour.

A.J. Toynbee

Society is produced by our wants and government by our wickedness.

Thomas Paine

Civilisation is a method of living, an attitude of equal respect for all men.

Jane Addams

> Civilisation –
> a heap of rubble scavenged by scrawny English Lit vultures.
> **Malcolm Muggeridge**

It is always possible to bind together a considerable number of people in love, so long as there are other people left over to receive the manifestations of their aggression.

Sigmund Freud

Society is like the air, necessary to breathe but insufficient to live on.

George Santayana

There can be hope only for a society which acts as one big family, not as many separate ones.

Anwar Sadat

In order to acquire a growing and lasting respect in society, it is a good thing, if you possess great talent, to give, early in your youth, a very hard kick to the right shin of the society that you love. After that, be a snob.

Salvador Dalí

Nature has never read the Declaration of Independence. It continues to make us unequal.

Will Durant

The most dangerous creation of any society is the man who has nothing to lose.

James Baldwin

Society is a masked ball, where everyone hides his real character, and reveals it by hiding.

Ralph Waldo Emerson

There is no such thing as society: there are individual men and women, and there are families. And no government can do anything except through people, and people must look after themselves first.

Margaret Thatcher

Society knows perfectly well how to kill a man and has methods more subtle than death.

André Gide

The history of all hitherto existing society is the history of class struggles.

Karl Marx

Every society honours its live conformists and its dead troublemakers.
Mignon McLaughlin

Never speak disrespectfully of society ... only people who can't get into it do that.

Oscar Wilde

KARL MARX

SIGMUND FREUD

MOTHER TERESA

ERNEST HEMINGWAY

P.G.

RICHARD BRANSON

F. SCOTT FITZGERALD

CHARLES DE GAULLE

W. SOMERSET MAUGHAM

PETER USTINOV

MICHELANGELO

EDDIE IZZARD

ALBERT CAMUS

ALAN BENNETT

GEORGE BERNARD

JOAN RIVERS

JONATHAN SWIFT

QUENTIN CRISP

W.H. AUDEN

MUHAMMAD ALI

DOLLY PARTON

JEAN-PAUL SARTRE

GEORGE ORWELL

WALT DISNEY

DOUGLAS ADAMS

JOHN F. KENNEDY

DOROTHY PARKER

ALBERT EINSTEIN

FRANK ZAPPA

NELSON MANDELA

OSCAR WILDE

MARGARET THATCHER

PABLO PICASSO AESOP
MARK TWAIN
WODEHOUSE BILL CLINTON
LEO TOLSTOY
ORSON WELLES
ISAAC ASIMOV
BUDDHA GROUCHO MARX
VIRGINIA WOOLF
JANE AUSTEN SAMUEL PEPYS
W.C. FIELDS MARILYN MONROE
SHAW MAE WEST
BERTRAND RUSSELL
BENJAMIN FRANKLIN
WINSTON CHURCHILL

THE CIRCLE OF LIFE

Birth
and babies

What is a home without children? Quiet.

Henny Youngman

A baby is God's opinion that the world should go on.

Carl Sandburg

It is not advisable to put your head around your child's door to see if it is asleep. It was.

Faith Hines

A child is helpless in inverse proportion to his age. He is at the zenith of his powers while he is an infant in arms. What on earth is more powerful than a very young baby?

Aline Kilmer

Our birth is nothing but our death begun.

Edward Young

A baby is nothing more than a loud noise at one end and no sense of responsibility at the other.

Ronald Knox

It takes three to make a birthday.

Penelope Leach

Death and taxes and childbirth. There's never any convenient time for any of them!

Margaret Mitchell

When your first baby drops its dummy, you sterilise it.
When your second baby drops its dummy, you tell the
dog to fetch.

Bruce Lansky

All babies are supposed to look like me – at both ends.

Winston Churchill

Don't buy one of those baby monitors. Babies pretend to
be dead. They're bastards and they do it on purpose.

Billy Connolly

If men had to have babies, they would only ever
have one each.

Diana, Princess of Wales

No matter what the ordinary person says, no matter who
it is that speaks, or what superlatives are employed, no baby
is admired sufficiently to please the mother.

E.V. Lucas

Babies are amazing. The way they stare into your eyes,
their exuberant smiles, how they begin each day all warm
and sleepy, smelling of promise. I suppose I never realised
it before, babies aren't really born of their parents, they're
born of every kind word, loving gesture, hope and dream
their parents ever had. Bliss.

Julia Roberts

People who say they sleep like a baby usually don't
have one.

Leo J. Burke

The first child is made of glass, the second porcelain,
the rest of rubber, steel and granite.

Richard J. Needham

No phallic hero, no matter what he does to himself or to
another to prove his courage, ever matches the solitary,
existential courage of the woman who gives birth.

Andrea Dworkin

There never was a child so lovely but his mother was
glad to get asleep.

Ralph Waldo Emerson

Humans are the only
animals that have
children on purpose –
with the exception
of guppies, who like
to eat theirs.

P.J. O'Rourke

The trouble with
children is that they
are not returnable.

Quentin Crisp

When I was a child

> A two year old is kind of like having a blender, but you don't have a top for it.
>
> **Jerry Seinfeld**

When I was a child, I spake as a child, I understood as a child, I thought as a child: but when I became a man, I put away childish things.

The Bible (I Corinthians)

Parents can only give good advice or put on the right paths, but the final forming of a person's character lies in their own hands.

Anne Frank

The quickest way for a parent to get a child's attention is to sit down and look comfortable.

Lane Olinghouse

Children should be seen and not smelt.

Joyce Jillson

Don't have any children. It makes divorce so much more complicated.

Albert Einstein

The real menace in dealing with a five year old is that in no time at all you begin to sound like a five year old.

Jean Kerr

Children **need love,** especially when they **do not deserve it.**

Harold S. Hulbert

Never have ideas about children, and never have ideas for them.

George Orwell

There is no end to the violations committed by children on children, quietly talking alone.

Elizabeth Bowen

The hardest job kids face today is learning good manners without seeing any.

Fred Astaire

If there is anything that we wish to change in a child, we should first examine it and see whether it is not something that could better be changed in ourselves.

Carl Jung

I've never outgrown that feeling of mild pride of acceptance, when children take your hand.

Ian McEwan

When childhood dies, its corpses are called adults.

Brian Aldiss

Watching your daughter being collected by her date feels like handing over a $1 million Stradivarius to a gorilla.

Jim Bishop

A happy childhood has spoiled many a promising life.

Robertson Davies

What music is more enchanting than the voices of young people, when you can't hear what they say?

Logan Pearsall Smith

You know that children are growing up when they start asking questions that have answers.

John J. Plomp

There are only two things a child will willingly share: communicable diseases and his mother's age.

Dr Benjamin Spock

One of the most obvious facts about grownups to a child is that they have forgotten what it is like to be a child.

Randall Jarrell

Children are not things to be moulded, but are people to be unfolded.

Jess Lair

A child is not a vase to be filled, but a fire to be lit.

François Rabelais

Every child is an artist. The problem is how to remain an artist once he grows up.

Pablo Picasso

If you want to see what children can do, you must stop giving them things.

Norman Douglas

School and education

Education's purpose is to replace an empty mind with an open one.
Malcolm Forbes

Education is the ability to listen to almost anything without losing your temper or your self-confidence.
Robert Frost

Education is learning what you didn't even know you didn't know.
Daniel J. Boorstin

Education is not preparation for life; education is life itself.
John Dewey

It is important that students bring a certain ragamuffin, barefoot irreverence to their studies; they are not here to worship what is known, but to question it.
Jacob Chanowski

A teacher affects eternity; he can never tell where his influence stops.
Henry Brooks Adams

That is the difference between good teachers and great teachers: good teachers make the best of a pupil's means; great teachers foresee a pupil's ends.
Maria Callas

Colleges hate geniuses, just as convents hate saints.
Ralph Waldo Emerson

The average Ph.D. thesis is nothing but a transference of bones from one graveyard to another.
J. Frank Dobie

What we become depends on what we read after all of the professors have finished with us. The greatest university of all is a collection of books.
Thomas Carlyle

The test of a good teacher is not how many questions he can ask his pupils that they will answer readily, but how many questions he inspires them to ask him which he finds it hard to answer.
Alice Wellington Rollins

Men are born ignorant, not stupid. They are made stupid by education.
Bertrand Russell

It is possible to store the mind with a million facts and still be entirely uneducated.

Alec Bourne

Education is the period during which you are being instructed by somebody you do not know, about something you do not want to know.

G.K. Chesterton

If you think education is expensive – try ignorance.

Derek Bok

Good teaching is one-fourth preparation and three-fourths theatre.

Gail Godwin

Education is the movement from darkness to light.

Allan Bloom

Education: that which reveals to the wise, and conceals from the stupid, the vast limits of their knowledge.

Mark Twain

A teacher is like a candle which lights others in consuming itself.

Giovanni Ruffini

Nothing in education is so astonishing as the amount of ignorance it accumulates in the form of inert facts.

Henry Brooks Adams

Education is like a double-edged sword. It may be turned to dangerous uses if it is not properly handled.

Wu Ting-Fang

What sculpture is to a block of marble, education is to the soul.

Joseph Addison

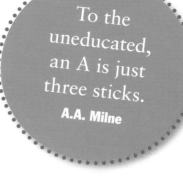

To the uneducated, an A is just three sticks.
A.A. Milne

The youth of today

Adolescence is the stage between puberty and adultery.

Denis Norden

Youth is the time to go flashing from one end of the world to the other both in mind and body; to try the manners of different nations; to hear the chimes at midnight.

Robert Louis Stevenson

When you are 17 you aren't really serious.

Arthur Rimbaud

How beautiful is youth! how bright it gleams
With its illusions, aspirations, dreams!
Book of beginnings, story without end,
Each maid a heroine, and each man a friend!

Henry Wadsworth Longfellow

The deepest definition of youth is life as yet untouched by tragedy.

Alfred North Whitehead

I remember my youth and the feeling that will never come back any more – the feeling that I could last for ever, outlast the sea, the earth and all men; the deceitful feeling that lures us on to joys, to perils, to love, to vain effort – to death; the triumphant conviction of strength, the heat of life in the handful of dust, the glow in the heart that with every year grows dim, grows cold, grows small, and expires – and expires, too soon, too soon – before death itself.

Joseph Conrad

It's better to **waste** one's youth than to do **nothing** with it at all.

Georges Courteline

Youth would be an ideal state if it came a little later in life.

Herbert Henry Asquith

Being young is greatly overestimated. Any failure seems so total. Later on you realise you can have another go.

Mary Quant

It were a real increase of human happiness, could all young men from the age of 19 be covered under barrels, or rendered otherwise invisible; and there left to follow their lawful studies and callings; till they emerged, sadder and wiser, at the age of 25.

Thomas Carlyle

I've never understood why people consider youth a time of freedom and joy. It's probably because they have forgotten their own.

Margaret Atwood

If I talk, everyone thinks I'm showing off; when I'm silent they think I'm ridiculous; rude if I answer; sly if I get a good idea, lazy if I'm tired, selfish if I eat a mouthful more than I should, stupid, cowardly, crafty, etc. etc.

Anne Frank

So much alarmed that she is quite alarming.
All Giggle, Blush, half Pertness, and half Pout.

Lord Byron

The young do not know enough to be prudent, and therefore they attempt the impossible – and achieve it, generation after generation.

Pearl S. Buck

There are three terrible ages of childhood – 1 to 10, 10 to 20, and 20 to 30.

Cleveland Amory

Youth is the only season for enjoyment, and the first 25 years of one's life are worth all the rest of the longest life of man, even though those five-and-twenty be spent in penury and contempt, and the rest in the possession of wealth, honours, respectability.

George Borrow

Youth is that period when a young boy knows everything but how to make a living.

Carey Williams

Teenage boys, goaded by their surging hormones, run in packs like the primal horde.

Camille Paglia

What Youth deemed crystal, Age finds out was dew.

Robert Browning

Adolescence is just one big walking pimple.
Carol Burnett

Rules for living

Life loves to be taken by the lapel and told, 'I'm with you, kid. Let's go.'

Maya Angelou

Follow the grain in your own wood.

Howard Thurman

Things in life will not always run smoothly. Sometimes we will be rising toward the heights – then all will seem to reverse itself and start downward. The great fact to remember is that the trend of civilisation itself is forever upward, that a line drawn through the middle of the peaks and the valleys of the centuries always has an upward trend.

Endicott Peabody

Stop acting as if life is a rehearsal. Live this day as if it were your last. The past is over and gone. The future is not guaranteed.

Wayne Dyer

Eliminate something superfluous from your life. Break a habit. Do something that makes you feel insecure.

Piero Ferrucci

If I had to live my life again, I'd make the same mistakes, only sooner.

Tallulah Bankhead

Think like a man of action, act like a man of thought.

Henri Bergson

You desire to know the art of living, my friend? It is contained in one phrase: make use of suffering.

Henri Frédéric Amiel

Live as if you were living a second time, and as though you had acted wrongly the first time.

Viktor E. Frankl

Go confidently in the direction of your dreams! Live the life you've imagined. As you simplify your life, the laws of the universe will be simpler.

Henry David Thoreau

In business or in life, don't follow the wagon tracks
too closely.

H. Jackson Brown

Realise deeply that the present moment is all you ever have.

Eckhart Tolle

Don't brood. Get on with living and loving. You don't
have forever.

Leo Buscaglia

Read, every day, something no one else is reading. Think,
every day, something no one else is thinking. Do, every day,
something no one else would be silly enough to do. It is bad
for the mind to be always part of unanimity.

Christopher Morley

A life spent making mistakes is not only more honourable
but more useful than a life spent in doing nothing.

George Bernard Shaw

See everything;
overlook a great
deal; correct
a little.
Pope John XXIII

You've got to **keep fighting** – you've got to
risk your life every six months to **stay
alive.**

Life is a great big canvas. Throw all the paint you can at it.

Danny Kaye

If you are going to ask yourself life-changing questions,
be sure to do something with the answers.

Bo Bennett

I have found that if you love life, life will love you back.

Arthur Rubinstein

Live as though it were your last day on earth. Some day
you will be right.

Robert Anthony

A man hath no better thing under the sun, than to eat,
and to drink, and to be merry.

The Bible (Ecclesiastes)

Enjoy life.
There's plenty of
time to be dead.

Hans Christian Andersen

Luck and opportunity

> Every exit is an entry somewhere.
>
> **Tom Stoppard**

One thing life has taught me: if you are interested, you never have to look for new interests. They come to you. When you are genuinely interested in one thing, it will always lead to something else.

Eleanor Roosevelt

The world is all gates, all opportunities, strings of tension waiting to be struck.

Ralph Waldo Emerson

A wise man will make more opportunities than he finds.

Francis Bacon

Luck? I don't know anything about luck. I've never banked on it and I'm afraid of people who do. Luck to me is something else: hard work – and realising what is opportunity and what isn't.

Lucille Ball

Luck is what you have left over after you give 100 per cent.

Langston Coleman

The world is round and the place which may seem like the end may also be only the beginning.

Ivy Baker Priest

Some folk want their luck buttered.

Thomas Hardy

We are continually faced with a series of great opportunities brilliantly disguised as insoluble problems.

John W. Gardner

The cards are ill shuffled till I have a good hand.

Jonathan Swift

Chance is always powerful. Let your hook be always cast; in the pool where you least expect it, there will be a fish.

Ovid

The only sure thing about luck is that it will change.

Bret Harte

Opportunity dances with those already on the dance floor.

H. Jackson Brown

Those who trust to chance must abide by the results of chance.

Calvin Coolidge

In the field of observation, chance favours only the prepared mind.

Louis Pasteur

Life is like a game of cards. The hand that is dealt you is determinism; the way you play it is free will.

Jawaharlal Nehru

The Chinese use two brush strokes to write the word crisis. One brush stroke stands for danger; the other for opportunity. In a crisis, be aware of the danger – but recognise the opportunity.

Richard M. Nixon

People always call it luck when you've acted more sensibly than they have.

Anne Tyler

Opportunity is missed by most people because it is dressed in overalls and looks like work.

Thomas Alva Edison

Shallow men believe in luck. Strong men believe in cause and effect.

Ralph Waldo Emerson

Luck is not something you can mention in the presence of self-made men.

E.B. White

If your ship doesn't come in, swim out to it!

Jonathan Winters

We must believe in luck. For how else can we explain the success of those we don't like?

Jean Cocteau

We must beat the iron while it is hot, but we may polish it at leisure.

John Dryden

> Success is simply a matter of luck. Ask any failure.
>
> **Earl Wilson**

Aims and goals

> To achieve great things, two things are needed: a plan, and not quite enough time.
>
> **Leonard Bernstein**

> There are many paths to the top of the mountain, but only one view.
>
> **Harry Millner**

Aim at the sun, and you may not reach it; but your arrow will fly far higher than if aimed at an object on a level with yourself.

Joel Hawes

Arriving at one goal is the starting point to another.

Fedor Dostoevsky

The question should be 'Is it worth trying to do?' – not, 'Can it be done?'

Allard Lowenstein

The reason most people never reach their goals is that they don't define them, or ever seriously consider them as believable or achievable. Winners can tell you where they are going, what they plan to do along the way, and who will be sharing the adventure with them.

Denis Watley

Be like a postage stamp. Stick to one thing until you get there.

Josh Billings

We succeed only as we identify in life, or in war, or in anything else, a single overriding objective, and make all other considerations bend to that one objective.

Dwight D. Eisenhower

Make no little plans; they have no magic to stir men's blood ... Make big plans, aim high in hope and work.

Daniel H. Burnham

I am extraordinarily patient provided I get my own way in the end.

Margaret Thatcher

The indispensable first step to getting the things you want out of life is this: decide what you want.

Ben Stein

A goal without a plan is just a wish.

Antoine de Saint-Exupéry

Nothing contributes so much to tranquillising the mind as a steady purpose – a point on which the soul may fix its intellectual eye.

Mary Shelley

An ant on the move does more than a dozing ox.

Lao-Tzu

A successful individual typically sets his next goal somewhat but not too much above his last achievement. In this way he steadily raises his level of aspiration.

Kurt Lewin

Whoever wants to reach a distant goal must take small steps.

Saul Bellow

Take time to deliberate, but when the time for action has arrived, stop thinking and go in.

Napoleon Bonaparte

Establishing goals is all right if you don't let them deprive you of interesting detours.

Doug Larson

The discipline you learn and character you build from setting and achieving a goal can be more valuable than the achievement of the goal itself.

Bo Bennett

Have no fear of perfection: you'll never reach it.

Salvador Dalí

When people are put into positions **slightly above** what they would **expect**, they're apt to excel.

Richard Branson

We must be willing to get rid of the life we've planned, so as to have the life that is waiting for us.

Joseph Campbell

Nelson Mandela

FATHER OF THE RAINBOW NATION

His life devoted to combating the racist apartheid regime of South Africa has made Nelson Mandela probably the most recognised and respected man on the planet. A large portion of that life, 27 long years, were spent in prison. All that time he was completely out of sight of the wider world, but never forgotten.

In 1961, when he was 43, Mandela founded the armed wing of the African National Congress (ANC). This made him a terrorist in the eyes of the South African government. He was arrested, and sentenced to life imprisonment. At his trial in 1964 Mandela said 'I have dedicated myself to the struggle of the African people. I have cherished the ideal of a democratic and free society in which all persons live together in harmony and with equal opportunities. It is an ideal which I hope to achieve. But, if needs be, it is an ideal for which I am prepared to die.'

Mandela emerged from prison in 1990, as the apartheid regime was losing its grip on power. When free, multi-racial elections were held in 1994, the former prisoner was swept to the presidency of a new South Africa. Mandela was by then a smiling, fatherly symbol of hope and reconciliation – not just for the South African people or even for the African continent, but for the whole world.

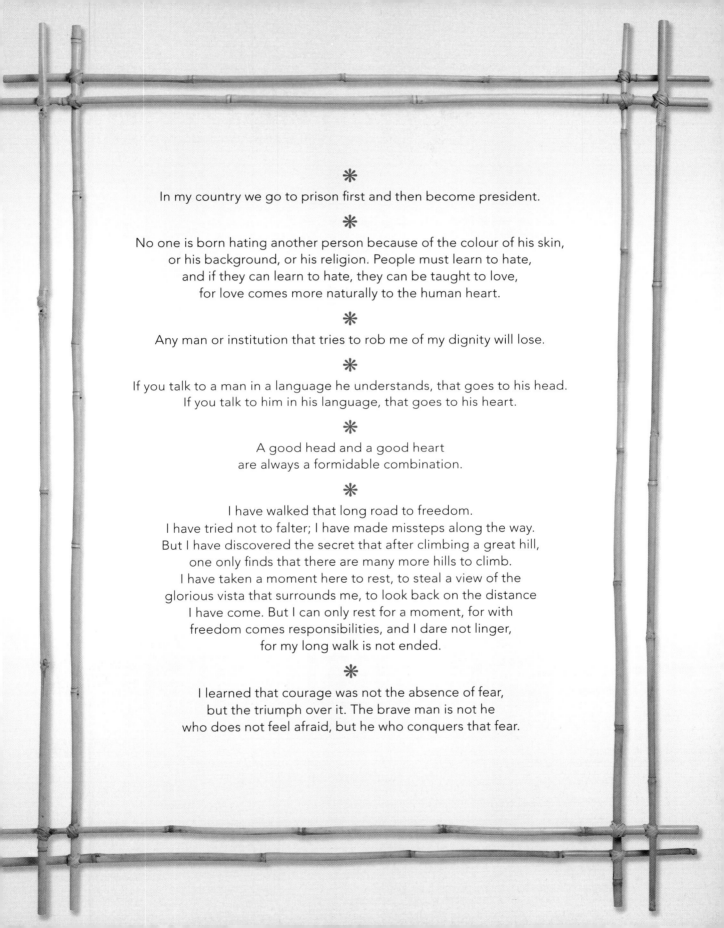

✳

In my country we go to prison first and then become president.

✳

No one is born hating another person because of the colour of his skin,
or his background, or his religion. People must learn to hate,
and if they can learn to hate, they can be taught to love,
for love comes more naturally to the human heart.

✳

Any man or institution that tries to rob me of my dignity will lose.

✳

If you talk to a man in a language he understands, that goes to his head.
If you talk to him in his language, that goes to his heart.

✳

A good head and a good heart
are always a formidable combination.

✳

I have walked that long road to freedom.
I have tried not to falter; I have made missteps along the way.
But I have discovered the secret that after climbing a great hill,
one only finds that there are many more hills to climb.
I have taken a moment here to rest, to steal a view of the
glorious vista that surrounds me, to look back on the distance
I have come. But I can only rest for a moment, for with
freedom comes responsibilities, and I dare not linger,
for my long walk is not ended.

✳

I learned that courage was not the absence of fear,
but the triumph over it. The brave man is not he
who does not feel afraid, but he who conquers that fear.

Choices and decisions

My friends, as I have discovered myself, there are no disasters, only opportunities. And, indeed, opportunities for fresh disasters.

Boris Johnson

One's mind has a way of making itself up in the background, and it suddenly becomes clear what one means to do.

A.C. Benson

You are remembered for the rules you break.

Douglas MacArthur

Informed decision-making comes from a long tradition of guessing and then blaming others for inadequate results.

Scott Adams

Once the what is decided, the how always follows. We must not make the how an excuse for not facing and accepting the what.

Pearl S. Buck

The hardest thing in life is to know which bridge to cross and which to burn.

David Russell

Sometimes when I consider what tremendous consequences come from little things, I am tempted to think there are no little things.

Bruce Barton

The man who insists on seeing with perfect clearness before he decides, never decides.

Henri Frédéric Amiel

There's small choice in rotten apples.

William Shakespeare

In any moment of decision the best thing you can do is the right thing, the next best thing is the wrong thing, and the worst thing you can do is nothing.

Theodore Roosevelt

Some persons are very decisive when it comes to avoiding decisions.

Brendan Francis

A weak man has doubts before a decision: a strong man has them afterwards.

Karl Kraus

Ever noticed that 'what the hell' is always the right decision?

Marilyn Monroe

You and I are essentially infinite choice-makers. In every moment of our existence, we are in that field of all possibilities where we have access to an infinity of choices.

Deepak Chopra

Decide promptly, but never give your reasons. Your decisions may be right, but your reasons are sure to be wrong.

Lord Mansfield

Later is always my first choice.

Mason Cooley

The man who is denied the opportunity of taking decisions of importance begins to regard as important the decisions he is allowed to take.

C. Northcote Parkinson

It is our choices that show what we truly are, far more than our abilities.

J.K. Rowling

There is no more miserable human being than one in whom nothing is habitual but indecision, and for whom the lighting of every cigar, the drinking of every cup, the time of rising and going to bed every day, and the beginning of every bit of work, are subjects of express volitional deliberation.

William James

You've got to make a conscious choice every day to shed the old – whatever the old means for you.

Sarah Ban Breathnach

Be willing to make decisions. That's the most important quality in a good leader. Don't fall victim to what I call the 'ready-aim-aim-aim-aim' syndrome. You must be willing to fire.

George S. Patton

We have to believe in free will. We've got no choice.

Isaac Bashevis Singer

He who hunts **two hares** leaves one and **loses the other.**

Japanese proverb

Making mistakes

> I have not failed.
> I've just found
> 10,000 ways that
> won't work.
>
> **Thomas Alva Edison**

Every great mistake has a halfway moment, a split second when it can be recalled and perhaps remedied.

Pearl S. Buck

We are built to make mistakes, coded for error.

Lewis Thomas

The follies which a man regrets the most, in his life, are those which he didn't commit when he had the opportunity.

Helen Rowland

Your best teacher is your last mistake.

Ralph Nader

The 50-50-90 rule: anytime you have a 50-50 chance of getting something right, there's a 90 per cent probability you'll get it wrong.

Andy Rooney

The only real mistake is the one from which we learn nothing.

John Powell

If all else fails, immortality can always be assured by spectacular error.

J.K. Galbraith

Mistakes are a part of being human. Appreciate your mistakes for what they are: precious life lessons that can only be learned the hard way. Unless it's a fatal mistake, which, at least, others can learn from.

Al Franken

You find out your mistakes from an audience that pays admission.

Edgar Bergen

If you live long enough, you'll make mistakes. But if you learn from them, you'll be a better person. It's how you handle adversity, not how it affects you. The main thing is never quit, never quit, never quit.

Bill Clinton

If we had more time for discussion we should probably have made a great many more mistakes.

Leon Trotsky

To swear off making mistakes is very easy. All you have to do is swear off having ideas.

Leo Burnett

Punishing honest mistakes stifles creativity. I want people moving and shaking the earth and they're going to make mistakes.

H. Ross Perot

It is necessary for us to learn from others' mistakes. You will not live long enough to make them all yourself.

Hyman G. Rickover

Not admiring a mistake is a bigger mistake.

Robert Half

Mistakes, obviously, show us what needs improving. Without mistakes, how would we know what we had to work on?

Peter McWilliams

He who never made a mistake, never made a discovery.

Samuel Smiles

You build on failure. You use it as a stepping stone. Close the door on the past. You don't try to forget the mistakes, but you don't dwell on it. You don't let it have any of your energy, or any of your time, or any of your space.

Johnny Cash

I beseech you, in the bowels of Christ, think it possible you may be mistaken.

Oliver Cromwell

A mistake is simply another way of doing things.

Katharine Graham

As she frequently remarked when she made any such mistake, it would be all the same a hundred years hence.

Charles Dickens

The man who makes no mistakes does not usually make anything.

Edward John Phelps

Mistakes are the portals of discovery.

James Joyce

The **light** of experience

A moment's insight is sometimes worth a life's experience.
Oliver Wendell Holmes

There is no wider gulf in the universe than yawns between those on the hither and thither side of vital experience.
Rebecca West

All experience is an arch to build upon.
Henry Brooks Adams

The only thing experience teaches us is that experience teaches us nothing.
André Maurois

Experience is the comb that nature gives us when we are bald.
Belgian proverb

Experience is not what happens to a man. It is what a man does with what happens to him.
Aldous Huxley

Experience is a good teacher, but she sends in terrific bills.
Minna Antrim

The light which experience gives is a lantern on the stern, which shines only on the waves behind us!
Samuel Taylor Coleridge

Never regret. If it's good, it's wonderful. If it's bad, it's **experience.**
Victoria Holt

Experience is a great spoiler of pleasures.
Mason Cooley

We come out of the dark and go into the dark again, and in between lie the experiences of our life.
Thomas Mann

I learned that one can never go back, that one should not ever try to go back – that the essence of life is going forward. Life is really a one-way street.
Agatha Christie

That which does not kill us makes us stronger.
Friedrich Nietzsche

Experience is a hard teacher because she gives the test first, the lesson afterwards.

Vernon Sanders Law

You should try everything once, except incest and morris dancing.

Thomas Beecham

Good judgment comes from experience, and experience comes from bad judgment.

Barry LePatner

Experience teaches only the teachable.

Aldous Huxley

As experience widens, one begins to see how much upon a level all human things are.

Joseph Farrell

Human beings, who are almost unique in having the ability to learn from the experience of others, are also remarkable for their apparent disinclination to do so.

Douglas Adams

Experience was of no ethical value. It was merely the name men gave to their mistakes.

Oscar Wilde

The trouble with learning from experience is that you never graduate.

Doug Larson

All growth is a leap in the dark, a spontaneous unpremeditated act without the benefit of experience.

Henry Miller

What one has not experienced, one will never understand in print.

Isadora Duncan

The **middle** years

> You grow up the day you have the first real laugh at yourself.
> **Ethel Barrymore**

Age is a question of mind over matter. If you don't mind, it doesn't matter.

Satchel Paige

Age is no guarantee of maturity.

Lawana Blackwell

To be mature means to face, and not evade, every fresh crisis that comes.

Fritz Kunkel

Maturity begins to grow when you can sense your concern for others outweighing your concern for yourself.

John MacNaughton

I have a problem about being nearly 60: I keep waking up in the morning and thinking I'm 31.

Elizabeth Janeway

True maturity is only reached when a man realises he has become a father figure to his girlfriends' boyfriends – and he accepts it.

Larry McMurtry

Age is a high price to pay for maturity.

Tom Stoppard

The really frightening thing about middle age is that you know you'll grow out of it.

Doris Day

Middle age is when you've met so many people that every new person you meet reminds you of someone else.

Ogden Nash

Setting a good example for children takes all the fun out of middle age.

William Feather

Middle age is when your broad mind and narrow waist begin to change places.

E. Joseph Crossman

After 30, a body has a mind of its own.

Bette Midler

Middle age is that perplexing time of life when we hear two voices calling us, one saying, 'Why not?' and the other, 'Why bother?'

Sydney J. Harris

Middle age occurs when you are too young to take up golf and too old to rush up to the net.

Franklin P. Adams

Everybody my age should be issued with a 2lb fresh salmon. If you see someone young, beautiful and happy, you should slap them as hard as you can with it.

Richard Griffiths

The man who views the world at 50 the same as he did at 20 has wasted 30 years of his life.

Muhammad Ali

Another belief of mine: that everyone else my age is an adult, whereas I am merely in disguise.

Margaret Atwood

Forty is the old age of youth; fifty is the youth of old age.

Victor Hugo

Imagination grows by exercise, and contrary to common belief, is more powerful in the mature than in the young.

W. Somerset Maugham

Whenever the talk turns to age, I say I am 49 plus VAT.

Lionel Blair

By the time you hit 50, I reckon you've earned your wrinkles, so why not be proud of them?

Twiggy

I am past 30, and three parts iced over.

Matthew Arnold

My best birth control now is just to leave the lights on.
Joan Rivers

Boys will be boys, and so will a lot of middle-aged men.
Kin Hubbard

Winning and losing

> Show me someone without an ego, and I'll show you a loser.
> **Donald Trump**

Never ascribe to an opponent motives meaner than your own.

J.M. Barrie

Nice guys finish last, but we get to sleep in.

Evan Davis

The minute you start talking about what you're going to do if you lose, you have lost.

George Shultz

Never confuse a single defeat with a final defeat.

F. Scott Fitzgerald

In real life, it is the hare who wins. Every time. Look around you. And in any case it is my contention that Aesop was writing for the tortoise market. Hares have no time to read. They are too busy winning the game.

Anita Brookner

The moment of victory is much too short to live for that and nothing else.

Martina Navratilova

If you don't win, you're going to be fired. If you do win, you've only put off the day you're going to be fired.

Leo Durocher

Show me a guy who's afraid to look bad, and I'll show you a guy you can beat every time.

Lou Brock

Try again. Fail again. Fail better.

Samuel Beckett

One should always play fairly when one has the winning cards.

Oscar Wilde

For when the One Great Scorer comes
To write against your name,
He marks – not that you won or lost –
But how you played the game.

Grantland Rice

Even victors are by victories undone.

John Dryden

When you win, say nothing. When you lose,
say less.

Paul Brown

There is nothing to winning, really. That is, if you
happen to be blessed with a keen eye, an agile mind,
and no scruples whatsoever.

Alfred Hitchcock

A winner never whines.

Paul Brown

What would you attempt to do if you knew you
could not fail?

Robert Schuller

The will to win is important, but the will to prepare is vital.

Joe Paterno

Win as if you were used to it, lose as if you enjoyed it
for a change.

Ralph Waldo Emerson

The only way to prove that you're a good sport is to lose.

Ernie Banks

The important thing in life is not the victory but the contest;
the essential thing is not to have won but to have fought well.

Baron Pierre de Coubertin

I'd kill for a Nobel Peace Prize.

Steven Wright

Everybody has won, and all must have prizes.

Lewis Carroll

**If winning isn't
everything, why do
they keep score?**
Vince Lombardi

Slow and steady
wins the race.
Aesop

Quentin Crisp

GLAD TO BE GAY

One of the most admirable things about writer, wit and raconteur Quentin Crisp is that he was so generous with his personality. He never refused a dinner invitation, and he saw it as his duty to speak at length to all the complete strangers who called him on the phone. He was as interested in everybody as everybody was in him. 'Idleness is my only occupation,' he said. 'And people are my only hobby.'

It is hard now to grasp how dangerous it was, like Crisp, to be openly gay in Britain before the Second World War. As a young man in London, Crisp ('... reluctantly born on Christmas Day, 1908') was often attacked and abused for his sexuality, but he always had the courage to be himself. It was only in the 1970s, with the TV film version of his 1968 autobiography *The Naked Civil Servant*, that Crisp became widely known ('A pinch of notoriety will do,' he said), and by that time the old animosity towards homosexuality was on the wane. He became, as he put it, 'one of the stately homos of England'.

Crisp had blazed the trail for the next generation of gay men and women, and he had done it with immense grace and flamboyant good humour. He was selling himself short when he said that 'I seem to have become a latter-day Bernard Shaw – with all of the loquacity but none of the wisdom.'

✳
An autobiography is an obituary in serial form
with the last instalment missing.

✳
There is no need to do any housework at all.
After the first four years the dirt doesn't get any worse.

✳
Never keep up with the Joneses. Drag them down to your level.

✳
Health consists of having the same diseases as one's neighbours.

✳
The formula for achieving a successful relationship is simple:
you should treat all disasters as if they were trivialities
but never treat a triviality as if it were a disaster.

✳
It is not the simple statement of facts that ushers in
freedom; it is the constant repetition of them that
has this liberating effect. Tolerance is the result
not of enlightenment, but of boredom.

✳
Love is not enough. It must be the foundation, the
cornerstone – but not the complete structure.
It is much too pliable, too yielding.

✳
To know all is not to forgive all. It is to despise everybody.

Challenges and obstacles

> Great things are done when men and mountains meet.
> **William Blake**

Life is like walking along a crowded street – there always seem to be fewer obstacles to getting along on the opposite pavement – and yet, if one crosses over, matters are rarely mended.

Thomas H. Huxley

Circumstances hell! I make circumstances!

Bruce Lee

Try not to turn your life into a race, least of all an obstacle race.

José Bergamín

In every adversity there lies the seed of an equivalent advantage. In every defeat is a lesson showing you how to win the victory next time.

Robert Collier

There seems to be some perverse human characteristic that likes to make easy things difficult.

Warren Buffett

Each handicap is like a hurdle in a steeplechase, and when you ride up to it, if you throw your heart over, the horse will go along, too.

Lawrence Bixby

The way of the pioneer is always rough.

Harvey S. Firestone

The majority of men meet with failure because of their lack of persistence in creating new plans to take the place of those which fail.

Napoleon Hill

Be master of your petty annoyances and conserve your energies for the big, worthwhile things. It isn't the mountain ahead that wears you out – it's the grain of sand in your shoe.

Robert Service

The only use of an obstacle is to be overcome. All that an obstacle does with brave men is, not to frighten them, but to challenge them.

Woodrow Wilson

All the adversity I've had in my life, all my troubles and obstacles, have strengthened me ... You may not realise it when it happens, but a kick in the teeth may be the best thing in the world for you.

Walt Disney

You can't choose the ways in which you'll be tested.

Robert J. Sawyer

Challenges are what make life interesting; overcoming them is what makes life meaningful.

Joshua J. Marine

You've gotta find a way to get out of your own way, so you can progress in life.

Steve Carlton

We combat obstacles in order to get repose, and, when got, the repose is insupportable.

Henry Brooks Adams

If you can find a path with no obstacles, it probably doesn't lead anywhere.

Frank A. Clark

Adversity has the same effect on a man that severe training has on the pugilist: It reduces him to his fighting weight.

Josh Billings

Conceit is an insuperable obstacle to all progress.

Ellen Terry

A successful man is one who can lay a firm foundation with the bricks others have thrown at him.

David Brinkley

Impossible is a word to be found only in the dictionary of fools.
Napoleon Bonaparte

Growing old

Old age isn't so bad when you consider the alternative.
Maurice Chevalier

Growing old is like being increasingly penalised for a crime you haven't committed.

Anthony Powell

There is great consolation in getting old when you can remember well – but not too well. A great deal of the bitterness drops out of things then, and all the sweetness is left for the gathering.

Henry Lawson

To keep the heart unwrinkled, to be hopeful, kindly, cheerful, reverent – that is to triumph over old age.

Thomas Bailey Aldrich

All would live long, but none would be old.

Benjamin Franklin

Of all the self-fulfilling prophecies in our culture, the assumption that ageing means decline and poor health is probably the deadliest.

Marilyn Ferguson

The dead might as well try to speak to the living as the old to the young.

Willa Cather

A man is not **old** until regrets take **the place of dreams.**

John Barrymore

Age is not important unless you're a cheese.
Helen Hayes

One of the good things about getting older is you find you're more interesting than most of the people you meet.

Lee Marvin

You can judge your age by the amount of pain you feel when you come in contact with a new idea.

Pearl S. Buck

I look upon life as a gift from God. I did nothing to earn it. Now that the time is coming to give it back, I have no right to complain.

Joyce Cary

Cherish all your happy moments: they make a fine cushion for old age.

Christopher Morley

I used to dread getting older because I thought I would not be able to do all the things I wanted to do, but now that I am older I find that I don't want to do them.

Nancy Astor

We do not necessarily improve with age: for better or worse we become more like ourselves.

Peter Hall

It is not all bad, this getting old, ripening. After the fruit has got its growth it should juice up and mellow. God forbid I should live long enough to ferment and rot and fall to the ground in a squash.

Josh Billings

Just because there's snow on the roof, it doesn't mean the boiler has gone out.

Anon

It is very strange that the years teach us patience – that the shorter our time, the greater our capacity for waiting.

Elizabeth Taylor

Old age is the most unexpected of all things that happen to a man

Leon Trotsky

Men do not quit playing because they grow old; they grow old because they quit playing.

Oliver Wendell Holmes

I will never be an old man. To me, old age is always 15 years older than I am.

Bernard Baruch

Beautiful young people are accidents of nature, but beautiful old people are works of art.

Eleanor Roosevelt

Old age is like everything else. To make a success of it, you've got to start young.

Fred Astaire

The most distressing thing about old age is that the hangovers last longer.

Richard Harris

Time and tide

I wasted time, and now doth time waste me.

William Shakespeare

You are today where your thoughts have brought you; you will be tomorrow where your thoughts take you.

James Lane Allen

Never leave that till tomorrow which you can do today.

Benjamin Franklin

Never do today what you can put off till tomorrow. Delay may give clearer light as to what is best to be done.

Aaron Burr

Time is the coin of your life. It is the only coin you have, and only you can determine how it will be spent. Be careful lest you let other people spend it for you.

Carl Sandburg

Begin doing what you want to do now. We are not living in eternity. We have only this moment, sparkling like a star in our hand and melting like a snowflake. Let us use it before it is too late.

Marie Beynon Ray

Time enough to think about the future when you haven't any future to think of.

George Bernard Shaw

If we take care of the moments, the years will take care of themselves.

Maria Edgeworth

Suspect each moment, for it is a thief, tiptoeing away with more than it brings.

John Updike

Forever is composed of nows.

Emily Dickinson

Doing your best at this moment puts you in the best place for the next moment.

Oprah Winfrey

Avoiding the phrase 'I don't have time' will soon help you to realise that you do have the time needed for just about anything you choose to accomplish in life.

Bo Bennett

Regret for the things we did can be tempered by time;
it is regret for the things we did not do that is inconsolable.

Sydney J. Harris

The past is a source of knowledge, and the future
is a source of hope. Love of the past implies faith
in the future.

Stephen Ambrose

I look to the future because that's where I'm going to
spend the rest of my life.

George Burns

Three o'clock is always too late or too early for anything
you want to do.

Jean-Paul Sartre

Peace is when time doesn't matter as it passes by.

Maria Schell

I still find each day too short for all the thoughts
I want to think, all the walks I want to take,
all the books I want to read, and all the friends
I want to see.

John Burroughs

The future is like heaven – everyone exalts it,
but no one wants to go there now.

James Baldwin

Love the moment, and the energy of that moment
will spread beyond all boundaries.

Corita Kent

Eternity – waste of time.

Natalie Clifford Barney

Remember, today is the tomorrow you worried
about yesterday.

Dale Carnegie

Every instant of time is a pinprick of eternity.

Marcus Aurelius

Change and growth

> There's only one corner of the universe you can be certain of improving, and that's your own self.
>
> **Aldous Huxley**

There are things I can't force. I must adjust. There are times when the greatest change needed is a change of my viewpoint.

Denis Diderot

Life is like an ever-shifting kaleidoscope – a slight change, and all patterns alter.

Sharon Salzberg

Change will not come if we wait for some other person or some other time. We are the ones we've been waiting for. We are the change that we seek.

Barack Obama

Because things are the way they are, things will not stay the way they are.

Bertolt Brecht

What you are is what you have done, what you will be is what you do now.

Paul Roland

After you've done a thing the same way for two years, look it over carefully. After five years look at it with suspicion ... and after ten throw it away and start all over again.

Alfred Perlman

Everything flows, and nothing stays still. You can't step twice into the same river.

Heraclitus

Both tears and sweat are salty, but they render a different result. Tears will get you sympathy; sweat will get you change.

Jesse Jackson

Most of us are about as eager to be changed as we were to be born, and go through our changes in a similar state of shock.

James Baldwin

There is a certain relief in change, even though it be from bad to worse. It is often a comfort to shift one's position and be bruised in a new place.

Washington Irving

If you are distressed by anything external, the pain is not due to the thing itself, but to your estimate of it; and this you have the power to revoke at any moment.

Marcus Aurelius

Everything is connected ... no one thing can change by itself.
Paul Hawken

I have examined myself thoroughly and come to the conclusion that I don't need to change much.

Sigmund Freud

When you're **through changing,** you're **through**.
Bruce Barton

None of us knows what the next change is going to be, what unexpected opportunity is just around the corner, waiting a few months or a few years to change all the tenor of our lives.

Kathleen Norris

When we blindly adopt a religion, a political system, a literary dogma, we become automatons. We cease to grow.

Anaïs Nin

All conservatism is based upon the idea that if you leave things alone you leave them as they are. But you do not. If you leave a thing alone you leave it to a torrent of change.

G.K. Chesterton

Change your thoughts and you change your world.

Norman Vincent Peale

Without change, something sleeps inside us, and seldom awakens. The sleeper must awaken.

Frank Herbert

All appears to change when we change.

Henri Frédéric Amiel

Everyone thinks of changing the world, but no one thinks of changing himself.
Leo Tolstoy

Memorable

last **words**

If you are known for your wit and wisdom, you will want to make your final thoughts on this Earth count. Some great figures clearly prepared something weighty for the occasion, others ad-libbed brilliantly, while a number were simply caught unawares.

I've had a hell of a lot of fun and I've enjoyed every minute of it.
Errol Flynn

The ladies have to go first. Get in the lifeboat, to please me. Good-bye, dearie. I'll see you later.
John Jacob Astor (aboard the *Titanic*)

Friends, applaud; the comedy is finished.
Ludwig van Beethoven

Tell them I've had a wonderful life.
Ludwig Wittgenstein

Turn up the lights, I don't want to go home in the dark.
O. Henry

I have offended God and mankind because my work did not reach the quality it should have.
Leonardo da Vinci

It has all been very interesting.
Lady Mary Wortley Montagu

Goodnight my darlings, I'll see you tomorrow.
Noël Coward

If this is dying, then I don't think much of it.
Lytton Strachey

Too late for fruit, too soon for flowers.
Walter De La Mare

I must go in, the fog is rising.
Emily Dickinson

Go on, get out – last words are for fools who haven't said enough.
Karl Marx

Everybody has got to die, but I have always believed an exception would be made in my case. Now what?
William Saroyan

I am not the least afraid to die.
Charles Darwin

I am just going outside and may be some time.
Lawrence Oates

You can keep the things of bronze and stone and give me one man to remember me just once a year.
Damon Runyon

My design is to make what haste I can to be gone.
Oliver Cromwell

I have a long journey to take, and must bid the company farewell.
Walter Raleigh (at his execution)

I feel nothing, except a certain difficulty in continuing to exist.
Bernard de Fontenelle

The **final** curtain

> Death is
> the sound of
> distant thunder
> at a picnic.
> **W.H. Auden**

At the end of your life, you will never regret not having passed one more test, not winning one more verdict or not closing one more deal. You will regret time not spent with a husband, a friend, a child, or a parent.

Barbara Bush

The bitterest tears shed over graves are for words left unsaid and deeds left undone.

Harriet Beecher Stowe

I do not believe that any man fears to be dead, but only the stroke of death.

Francis Bacon

Dying is an art, like everything else.

Sylvia Plath

Death is nothing, but to live defeated and inglorious is to die daily.

Napoleon Bonaparte

Once they tell you you're in God's hands, you know you're done.

Alan Marshall

I detest life-insurance agents; they always argue that I shall some day die, which is not so.

Stephen Leacock

Life is **pleasant.** Death is **peaceful.** It's the transition that's **troublesome**.

Isaac Asimov

If even dying is to be made a social function, then, please, grant me the favour of sneaking out on tiptoe without disturbing the party.

Dag Hammarskjöld

It's not that I'm afraid to die. I just don't want to be there when it happens.

Woody Allen

The key to dying well is for you to decide where, when, how and whom to invite to the last party.

Timothy Leary

One dies only once, and it's for such a long time!

Molière

Life is a great surprise. I do not see why death should not be an even greater one.

Vladimir Nabokov

The bodies of those that made such a noise and tumult when alive, when dead, lie as quietly among the graves of their neighbours as any others.

Jonathan Edwards

Death must be distinguished from dying, with which it is often confused.

Sydney Smith

For three days after death, hair and fingernails continue to grow but phone calls taper off.

Johnny Carson

If there wasn't death, I think you couldn't go on.

Stevie Smith

I'm terrified of dying in a plane crash. I hate the thought that peanuts would be my last meal.

Tanya Luckerath

Life is like a B-movie. You don't want to leave in the middle of it, but you don't want to see it again either.

Ted Turner

If I die before my cat, I want some of my ashes put in his food so I can live on inside him.

Drew Barrymore

Anyone can stop a man's life, but no one his death; a thousand doors open on to it.

Seneca

Death is nature's way of telling you to slow down.

Anon

Death is a very dull, dreary affair. And my advice to you is to have nothing whatsoever to do with it.

W. Somerset Maugham

Do not fear death so much, but rather the inadequate life.

Bertolt Brecht

The **nature** of existence

Oh, isn't life a terrible thing, thank God?
Dylan Thomas

Life is like playing a violin solo in public and learning the instrument as one goes on.
Edward Bulwer-Lytton

When one subtracts from life infancy (which is vegetation), – sleep, eating and swilling – buttoning and unbuttoning – how much remains of downright existence? The summer of a dormouse.
Lord Byron

People say that life is the thing, but I prefer reading.
Logan Pearsall Smith

Life is what happens to you while you're busy making other plans.
Anon

You only live once – but if you work it right, once is enough.
Joe E. Lewis

Learning to live what you're born with is the process, the involvement, the making of a life.
Diane Wakoski

Life's a voyage that's homeward bound.
Herman Melville

Life can only be understood backwards; but it must be lived forwards.
Søren Kierkegaard

Life's a tough proposition, and the first hundred years are the hardest.
Wilson Mizner

The way I see it, if you want the rainbow you gotta put up with the rain.
Dolly Parton

The living are just the dead on holiday.

Maurice Maeterlinck

When I hear somebody sigh 'Life is hard' I am always tempted to ask 'Compared to what?'

Sydney J. Harris

Every man's life is a fairy tale written by God's fingers.

Hans Christian Andersen

It is said an eastern monarch once charged his wise men to invent a sentence, to be ever in view, and which should be true and appropriate in all times and situations. They presented him with the words, 'And this, too, shall pass away.' How much it expresses! How chastening in the hour of pride! How consoling in the depths of affliction!

Abraham Lincoln

Everything has been figured out, except how to live.

Jean-Paul Sartre

The tragedy of life is not that it ends so soon, but that we wait so long to begin it.

W.M. Lewis

Life isn't fair.
It's just fairer than
death, that's all.
William Goldman

Life is hardly more than a **fraction** of a **second.** Such a little time to prepare oneself for **eternity!**

Paul Gauguin

To be able to look back upon one's past life with satisfaction is to live twice.

Lord Acton

Life is a moderately good play with a badly written third act.

Truman Capote

No arts; no letters; no society; and which is worst of all, continual fear and danger of violent death; and the life of man, solitary, poor, nasty, brutish and short.

Thomas Hobbes

That's the trouble with life – crap dialogue and bad lighting.

Elizabeth Taylor

KARL MARX

SIGMUND FREUD

MOTHER TERESA

F. SCOTT FITZGERALD

ERNEST HEMINGWAY

P.G.

RICHARD BRANSON

CHARLES DE GAULLE

W. SOMERSET MAUGHAM

PETER USTINOV

MICHELANGELO

EDDIE IZZARD

ALBERT CAMUS

ALAN BENNETT

GEORGE BERNARD

JOAN RIVERS

JONATHAN SWIFT

QUENTIN CRISP

W.H. AUDEN

MUHAMMAD ALI

DOLLY PARTON

JEAN-PAUL SARTRE

GEORGE ORWELL

WALT DISNEY

DOUGLAS ADAMS

JOHN F. KENNEDY

DOROTHY PARKER

ALBERT EINSTEIN

FRANK ZAPPA

NELSON MANDELA

OSCAR WILDE

MARGARET THATCHER

PABLO PICASSO AESOP

MARK TWAIN

LEO TOLSTOY

ORSON WELLES

ISAAC ASIMOV

BUDDHA GROUCHO MARX

WODEHOUSE BILL CLINTON

VIRGINIA WOOLF

JANE AUSTEN SAMUEL PEPYS

W.C. FIELDS MARILYN MONROE

SHAW MAE WEST

BERTRAND RUSSELL

MIND
AND SPIRIT

You
and your Self

No one can make you feel inferior without your consent.

Eleanor Roosevelt

I wish I was what I used to be when I wished I was what I am.

Anon

There are two types of people – those who come into a room and say 'Well, here I am!' and those who come in and say 'Ah, there you are.'

Frederick L. Collins

Self-esteem is the reputation we acquire with ourselves.

Nathaniel Branden

I define comfort as self-acceptance. When we finally learn that self-care begins and ends with ourselves, we no longer demand sustenance and happiness from others.

Jennifer Louden

Avoid the crowd. Do your own thinking independently. Be the chess player, not the chess piece.

Ralph Charell

Faith in oneself is the best and safest course.

Michelangelo

How can you come to know yourself? Never by thinking, always by doing. Try to do your duty, and you'll know right away what you amount to.

Johann Wolfgang von Goethe

We are all special cases.

Albert Camus

Trust yourself. Think for yourself. Act for yourself. Speak for yourself. Be yourself. Imitation is suicide.

Marva Collins

I've learned my song, and I sing it.

Bob Barker

The thing that is really hard, and really amazing, is giving up on being perfect and beginning the work of becoming yourself.

Anna Quindlen

Everyone is necessarily the hero of his own life story.

John Barth

If egotism means a terrific interest in one's self, egotism is absolutely essential to efficient living.

Arnold Bennett

The living self has one purpose only: to come into its own fullness of being, as a tree comes into blossom, or a bird into spring beauty, or a tiger into lustre.

D.H. Lawrence

Knowing others is intelligence; knowing yourself is true wisdom. Mastering others is strength, mastering yourself is true power.

Lao-Tzu

Do not be awestruck by other people and try to copy them. Nobody can be you as efficiently as you can.

Norman Vincent Peale

Each has his past shut in him like the leaves of a book known to him by heart and his friends can only read the title.

Virginia Woolf

Were it not for myself, I should get along quite well.

Alphonse Karr

Never feel self-pity, the most destructive emotion there is. How awful to be caught up in the terrible squirrel cage of self.

Millicent Fenwick

I have always disliked myself at any given moment. The total of such moments is my life.

Cyril Connolly

Sometimes you have to play for a long time to be able to play like yourself.
Miles Davis

Always be a first-rate version of yourself, instead of a second-rate version of somebody else.

Judy Garland

Be happy!

Happiness is neither virtue nor pleasure nor this thing nor that but simply growth. We are happy when we are growing.

W.B. Yeats

The joy that isn't shared dies young.

Anne Sexton

Happiness is different from pleasure. Happiness has something to do with struggling and enduring and accomplishing.

George Sheehan

It is the paradox of life that the way to miss pleasure is to seek it first. The very first condition of lasting happiness is that a life should be full of purpose, aiming at something outside self.

Hugo Black

It is not easy to find happiness in ourselves, and it is not possible to find it elsewhere.

Agnes Repplier

There are lots of ways of being miserable, but there's only one way of being comfortable, and that is to stop running round after happiness. If you make up your mind not to be happy there's no reason why you shouldn't have a fairly good time.

Edith Wharton

The grand essentials of happiness are: something to do, something to love, and something to hope for.

Allan K. Chalmers

There will always be a lost dog somewhere that will prevent me from being happy.

Jean Anouilh

I don't think everyone has the right to happiness or to be loved. Even the Americans have written into their constitution that you have the right to the 'pursuit of happiness'. You have the right to try – but that is all.

Claire Rayner

The happiest women, like the happiest nations, have no history.

George Eliot

People take different roads seeking fulfilment and happiness. Just because they're not on your road doesn't mean they've gotten lost.

H. Jackson Brown

Fundamental happines depends more than anything else upon what may be called a friendly interest in persons and things.

Bertrand Russell

No one is in control of your happiness but you; therefore, you have the power to change anything about yourself or your life that you want to change.

Barbara De Angelis

Happiness is as a butterfly which, when pursued, is always beyond our grasp, but which if you will sit down quietly, may alight upon you.

Nathaniel Hawthorne

This lamentable phrase 'the pursuit of happiness' is responsible for a good part of the ills and miseries of the modern world.

Malcolm Muggeridge

When one door of happiness closes, another opens; but often we look so long at the closed door that we do not see the one which has opened for us.

Helen Keller

> One of the keys to happiness is a bad memory.
> **Rita Mae Brown**

Nobody really cares if you're miserable, so you might as well be happy.
Cynthia Nelms

I have **no money, no resources, no hopes.** I am the happiest man alive.

Henry Miller

There can be no happiness if the things we believe in are different from the things we do.

Freya Stark

If your happiness depends on what somebody else does, I guess you do have a problem.

Richard Bach

We have no more right to consume happiness without producing it than to consume wealth without producing it.

George Bernard Shaw

and desires

Some men see things as they are and ask 'Why?'; I dream things that never were and ask 'Why not?'

Robert F. Kennedy

I'm not a dreamer … but I believe in miracles. I have to.

Terry Fox

Believe me, of all the people in the world, those who want the most are those who have the most.

David Grayson

Suffering is caused by desire.

Buddha

Our subconscious minds have no sense of humour, play no jokes and cannot tell the difference between reality and an imagined thought or image. What we continually think about eventually will manifest in our lives.

Robert Collier

We grow great by dreams. All big men are dreamers.

Woodrow Wilson

Nothing is as real as a dream. The world can change around you, but your dream will not. Responsibilities need not erase it. Duties need not obscure it. Because the dream is within you, no one can take it away.

Tom Clancy

We would often be sorry if our wishes were gratified.

Aesop

Those who dream by day are cognisant of many things which escape those who dream only by night.

Edgar Allan Poe

Desire is the very essence of man.

Baruch Spinoza

Boredom: the desire for desires.

Leo Tolstoy

Each man is given, in dreams, a little personal eternity which allows him to see the recent past and the near future.

Jorge Luis Borges

Illusions com mend themselves to us because they save us pain and allow us to enjoy pleasure instead. We must therefore accept it without complaint when they sometimes collide with a bit of reality against which they are dashed to pieces.

Sigmund Freud

The dreams of reason produce monsters.

Goya

We are all kings and conquerors in the silent empire of our fantasies.

Smiley Blanton

A man has more fun wishing for the things he hasn't got than enjoying the things he has got.

Finley Peter Dunne

Follow your bliss and doors will open where there were no doors before.

Joseph Campbell

Want a thing long enough, and you don't.

Chinese proverb

Our desires attract supporting reasons as a magnet the iron filings.

W. Macneile Dixon

All our dreams can come true, if we have the courage to pursue them.
Walt Disney

The desires of **the heart** are as **crooked** as corkscrews.

W.H. Auden

Optimism and pessimism

Since I gave up hope, I feel so much better.

John Osborne

No pessimist ever discovered the secret of the stars, or sailed to an uncharted land, or opened a new doorway for the human spirit.

Helen Keller

The optimist proclaims that we live in the best of all possible worlds; and the pessimist fears this is true.

James Branch Cabell

One has to have the courage of one's pessimism.

Ian McEwan

Many an optimist has become rich by buying out a pessimist.

Robert G. Allen

Pessimists are not boring. Pessimists are right. Pessimists are superfluous.

Elias Canetti

Our attitudes control our lives. Attitudes are a secret power working 24 hours a day, for good or bad. It is of paramount importance that we know how to harness and control this great force.

Irving Berlin

Things turn out best for the people who make the best of the way things turn out.

Art Linkletter

Pessimism is depreciated will-to-live.

Albert Schweitzer

A strong positive mental attitude will create more miracles than any wonder drug.

Patricia Neal

The light at the end of the tunnel is just the light of an oncoming train.

Robert Lowell

I have become my own version of an optimist. If I can't make it through one door, I'll go through another door – or I'll make a door. Something terrific will come no matter how dark the present.

Joan Rivers

The basis of optimism is sheer terror.

Oscar Wilde

Expect the best. Prepare for the worst. Capitalise on what comes.

Zig Ziglar

Don't ever become a pessimist … A pessimist is correct oftener than an optimist, but an optimist has more fun, and neither can stop the march of events.

Robert A. Heinlein

I never saw a pessimistic general win a battle.

Dwight D. Eisenhower

Nothing is more dangerous than ill-founded optimism; in the end it can produce only despair.

Henri de Lubac

Stick with the optimists. It's going to be tough enough even if they're right.

James Reston

Pessimism, when you get used to it, is just as agreeable as optimism. Indeed, I think it must be more agreeable, must have a more real savour, than optimism – from the way in which pessimists abandon themselves to it.

Arnold Bennett

Optimism is the opium of the people.

Milan Kundera

The lark's on the wing;
The snail's on the thorn:
God's in his heaven –
All's right with the world!

Robert Browning

> A pessimist is one who makes difficulties of his opportunities and an optimist is one who makes opportunities of his difficulties.
>
> **Harry S Truman**

I am an optimist. It does not seem too much use being anything else.

Winston Churchill

> Both optimists and pessimists contribute to society. The optimist invents the aeroplane, the pessimist the parachute.
>
> **George Bernard Shaw**

Ideas and insights

It is only with the heart that one can see rightly;
what is essential is invisible to the eye.

Antoine de Saint-Exupéry

Man is ready to die for an idea, provided that idea is
not quite clear to him.

Paul Eldridge

An idea isn't responsible for the
people who believe in it.

Don Marquis

Nothing is more dangerous
than an idea, when you have
only one.

Emile-Auguste Chartier

Sometimes the best, and only effective, way to kill an
idea is to put it into practice.

Sydney J. Harris

Beware when the great God lets loose a thinker
on this planet.

Ralph Waldo Emerson

The human mind treats a new idea the same way the
body treats a strange protein; it rejects it.

P.B. Medawar

No man can describe how an idea comes to him.

Isaac Bashevis Singer

If the doors of perception were cleansed everything would
appear to man as it is, infinite.
For man has closed himself up, till he sees all things thro'
narrow chinks of his cavern.

William Blake

If everyone says you are wrong, you're one step ahead.
If everyone laughs at you, you're two steps ahead.

Charles 'Chic' Thompson

There are some ideas
so wrong that only a
very intelligent person
could believe in them.

George Orwell

New opinions are always suspected, and usually
opposed, without any other reason but because they
are not already common.

John Locke

Do not fear to be eccentric in opinion, for every opinion now accepted was once eccentric.

Bertrand Russell

Any philosophy that can be put in a nutshell belongs there.

Sydney J. Harris

It is better to entertain an idea than to take it home to live with you for the rest of your life.

Randall Jarrell

The greatest ideas seem meagre enough when they have passed through the sieve of petty minds.

Henri de Lubac

As soon as an idea is accepted it is time to reject it.

Holbrook Jackson

Except by illustrations drawn from familiar things, there is no way of indicating a new idea.

Richard Jefferies

I share no one's ideas. I have my own.

Ivan Turgenev

What matters is not the idea a man holds, but the depth at which he holds it.

Ezra Pound

Nothing dies harder than a bad idea.

Julia Cameron

Many ideas grow better when transplanted into another mind than in the one where they sprung up.

Oliver Wendell Holmes

The thinker dies, but his thoughts are beyond the reach of destruction. Men are mortal; but ideas are immortal.

Richard Adams

One sees great things from the valley; only small things from the peak.

G.K. Chesterton

The English approach to ideas is not to kill them, but to let them die of neglect.
Jeremy Paxman

Just my imagination

Put your talent
into your work,
but your genius
into your life.
Oscar Wilde

In every work of genuis, we recognise our own
rejected thoughts.

Ralph Waldo Emerson

Imagination grows by exercise and contrary to common
belief is more powerful in the mature than in the young.

W. Somerset Maugham

We know that the nature of genius is to provide idiots
with ideas 20 years later.

Louis Aragon

When a true genius appears in this world, you may
know him by this sign, that the dunces are all in
confederacy against him.

Jonathan Swift

The man who can't visualise a horse galloping on a tomato
is an idiot.

André Breton

Imagination isn't merely a surplus mental department meant
for entertainment, but the most essential piece of machinery
we have if we are going to live the lives of human beings.

Ted Hughes

By logic and reason
we die hourly; by
imagination we live.
John Butler Yeats

Imagination is more important than knowledge.

Albert Einstein

Use your imagination not to scare yourself to death but
to inspire yourself to life.

Adele Brookman

The imagination must be fed constantly by external
nature … The most imaginative men always study the
hardest, and are the most thirsty for new knowledge.

John Ruskin

Were it not for imagination, Sir, a man would be as happy
in the arms of a chambermaid as of a Duchess.

Samuel Johnson

There are lots of people who mistake their imagination for their memory.

Josh Billings

Genius is an infinite capacity for taking life by the scruff of the neck.

Christopher Quill

Every artist dips his brush in his own soul, and paints his own nature into his pictures.

Henry Ward Beecher

There is only one admirable form of the imagination: the imagination that is so intense that it creates a new reality, that it makes things happen.

Sean O'Faolain

Intelligence recognises what has happened. Genius recognises what will happen.

John Ciardi

Genius is nothing but a greater aptitude for patience.

George-Louis Leclerc de Buffon

One may have a blazing hearth in one's soul and yet no one ever comes to sit by it. Passers-by see only a wisp of smoke from the chimney and continue on the way.

Vincent van Gogh

Skill without imagination is craftsmanship and gives us many useful objects such as wickerwork picnic baskets. Imagination without skill gives us modern art.

Tom Stoppard

I cannot tell if genius is hereditary because heaven has granted me no offspring.

James McNeill Whistler

Martin Luther King, Jnr

MAN WITH A DREAM

He was born to preach – the son of a Baptist minister and himself the pastor of a church by the age of 25. But Martin Luther King, Jnr, achieved so much more in his short life, celebrated as the charismatic leader of America's black civil rights movement, a prophet of non-violence after the manner of Mahatma Gandhi, and the eloquent voice of an oppressed people.

The preacher from Atlanta, Georgia, came to prominence when he took over the leadership of the Alabama 'bus boycotts' in 1957. Over the next decade, by means of a series of brilliant campaigns, he undermined the system of racial segregation in the southern states of the USA. His 'I have a dream' speech made people of all races understand that the issue of African-American rights was one battle in humanity's long struggle for freedom and dignity.

King did not survive that battle: he was assassinated in 1968 in Memphis, Tennessee, at the age of 39. He seemed to sense that a violent death was nearing. The night before he was shot he made a speech in which he said: 'I don't know what will happen now. We've got some difficult days ahead. But it really doesn't matter with me now, because I've been to the mountaintop … I just want to do God's will, and He's allowed me to go up to the mountain. And I've looked over and I've seen the Promised Land. And I'm happy tonight; I'm not worried about anything. I'm not fearing any man.'

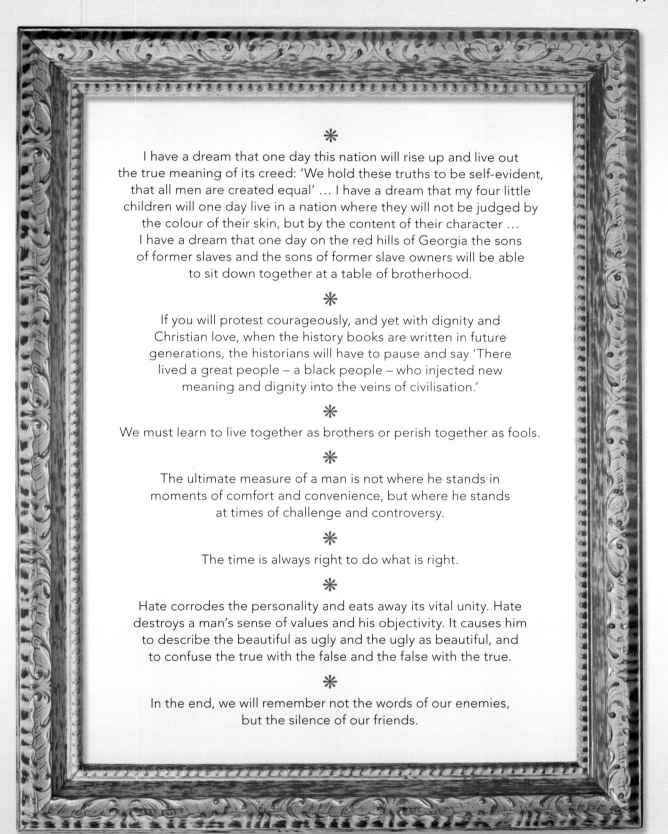

✳

I have a dream that one day this nation will rise up and live out
the true meaning of its creed: 'We hold these truths to be self-evident,
that all men are created equal' … I have a dream that my four little
children will one day live in a nation where they will not be judged by
the colour of their skin, but by the content of their character …
I have a dream that one day on the red hills of Georgia the sons
of former slaves and the sons of former slave owners will be able
to sit down together at a table of brotherhood.

✳

If you will protest courageously, and yet with dignity and
Christian love, when the history books are written in future
generations, the historians will have to pause and say 'There
lived a great people – a black people – who injected new
meaning and dignity into the veins of civilisation.'

✳

We must learn to live together as brothers or perish together as fools.

✳

The ultimate measure of a man is not where he stands in
moments of comfort and convenience, but where he stands
at times of challenge and controversy.

✳

The time is always right to do what is right.

✳

Hate corrodes the personality and eats away its vital unity. Hate
destroys a man's sense of values and his objectivity. It causes him
to describe the beautiful as ugly and the ugly as beautiful, and
to confuse the true with the false and the false with the true.

✳

In the end, we will remember not the words of our enemies,
but the silence of our friends.

Fate and destiny

I am a fatalist and believe that what will be, will; what is, is; and what was, was; and so on through the verbs.

Lennie Lower

He that is born to be hanged shall never be drowned.

French proverb

Nothing happens to anybody which he is not fitted by nature to bear.

Marcus Aurelius

Of course the game is rigged. Don't let that stop you – if you don't play, you can't win.

Robert A. Heinlein

The early bird gets the worm. The early worm … gets eaten.

Norman R. Augustine

No trumpets sound when the important decisions of our life are made. Destiny is made known silently.

Agnes de Mille

Destiny is an absolutely definite and inexorable ruler. Physical ability and moral determination count for nothing. It is impossible to perform the simplest act when the gods say no. I have no idea how they bring pressure to bear on such occasions; I only know that it is irresistible.

Aleister Crowley

If you don't run your own life, somebody else will.

John Atkinson

What do I know of man's destiny? I could tell you more about radishes.

Samuel Beckett

Ask many of us who are disabled what we would like in life and you would be surprised how few would say 'Not to be disabled'. We accept our limitations.

Itzhak Perlman

Destiny: a tyrant's authority for crime and a fool's
excuse for failure.

Ambrose Bierce

Two roads diverged in a wood, and I – I took the one less
travelled by. And that has made all the difference.

Robert Frost

I don't want to be a passenger in my own life.

Diane Ackerman

I do not believe in a fate that falls on men however they act;
but I do believe in a fate that falls on them unless they act.

G.K. Chesterton

Human beings have an inalienable right to invent themselves.

Germaine Greer

The gods, too, are fond of a joke.

Aristotle

We are no more free agents than the queen of clubs when
she victoriously takes prisoner the knave of hearts.

Lady Mary Wortley Montagu

Man is condemned to be free.

Jean-Paul Sartre

Destiny is not a matter of chance, it is a matter of choice;
it is not a thing to be waited for, it is a thing to be achieved.

William Jennings Bryan

I am not afraid of storms, for I am learning
how to sail my ship.

Louisa M. Alcott

We cannot direct
the wind, but
we can adjust
the sails.
Bertha Calloway

If you want a
guarantee, buy
a toaster.
Clint Eastwood

Faith and spirituality

> I knew it was going to be a bad day; my karma ran over my dogma.
> **Billy Connolly**

Preaching is to much avail, but practice is far more effective. A godly life is the strongest argument you can offer the sceptic.

Hosea Ballou

Nothing is so easy to fake as the inner vision.

Robertson Davies

Earth's crammed with heaven,
And every common bush afire with God;
But only he who sees, takes off his shoes;
The rest sit round it and pluck blackberries.

Elizabeth Barrett Browning

If God can work through me, he can work through anyone.

St Francis of Assisi

Faith moves mountains, but you have to keep pushing while you are praying.

Mason Cooley

The fact that I can plant a seed and it becomes a flower, share a bit of knowledge and it becomes another's, smile at someone and receive a smile in return, are to me continual spiritual exercises.

Leo Buscaglia

Faith is taking the first step even when you don't see the whole staircase.

Martin Luther King, Jnr

You don't have to be religious to have a soul; everybody has one. You don't have to be religious to perfect your soul; I have found saintliness in avowed atheists.

Harold S. Kushner

My religion is very simple. My religion is kindness.

Dalai Lama

Prayer: the Church's banquet, Angels' age,
God's breath in man returning to his birth,
The soul in paraphrase, heart in pilgrimage,
The Christian plummet, sounding heaven and earth …

George Herbert

'Tis not the dying for a faith that's so hard ... every man of every nation has done that – 'tis the living up to it that is difficult.

William Makepiece Thackeray

A belief is not merely an idea the mind possesses; it is an idea that possesses the mind.

Robert Bolton

Every charitable act is a stepping stone toward heaven.

Henry Ward Beecher

The wish to pray is a prayer in itself. God can ask no more than that of us.

Georges Bernanos

God knows that belief is more important than what we believe.

Elizabeth Bibesco

There is no need to go to India or anywhere else to find peace. You will find that deep place of silence right in your room, your garden or even your bathtub.

Elisabeth Kubler-Ross

Holiness is not the luxury of a few. It is everyone's duty, yours and mine.

Mother Teresa

Sudden prayers make God jump.

Eric Thacker and Anthony Earnshaw

We are always on the anvil; by trials God is shaping us for higher things.

Henry Ward Beecher

What is faith worth if it is not translated into action?

Mahatma Gandhi

Faith is not just something you have, it's something you do.

Barack Obama

The **Church** and religion

It is the test of a good religion whether you can joke about it.

G.K. Chesterton

Things have come to a pretty pass when religion is allowed to invade the sphere of private life.

Viscount Melbourne

As for the British churchman, he goes to church as he goes to the bathroom, with the minimum of fuss and no explanation if he can help it.

Ronald Blythe

He cannot have God as his father who refuses to have the Church for his mother.

St Augustine

Every religion is true one way or another. It is true when understood metaphorically. But when it gets stuck in its own metaphors, interpreting them as facts, then you are in trouble.

Joseph Campbell

My country is the world and my religion is to do good.

Thomas Paine

I am not a **pillar of the church** but a buttress – I **support** it from the outside.

Winston Churchill

I think vital religion has always suffered when orthodoxy is more regarded than virtue. The scriptures assure me that at the last day we shall not be examined on what we thought but what we did.

Benjamin Franklin

The test of every religious, political, or educational system is the man that it forms.

Henri Frédéric Amiel

Religion is the sigh of the oppressed creature, the heart of a heartless world, and the soul of soulless conditions. It is the opium of the people.

Karl Marx

I have observed that the world has suffered far less from ignorance than from pretensions to knowledge. It is not sceptics or explorers but fanatics and ideologues who menace decency and progress. No agnostic ever burned anyone at the stake or tortured a pagan, a heretic, or an unbeliever.

Daniel J. Boorstin

We must respect the other fellow's religion, but only in the sense and to the extent that we respect his theory that his wife is beautiful and his children smart.

H.L. Mencken

You have to be very religious to change your religion.

Comtesse Diane

Treat the other man's faith gently; it is all he has to believe with. His mind was created for his own thoughts, not yours or mine.

Henry S. Haskins

No great religion was ever a wholly new religion. Christianity could hardly have made its universal appeal if it had not taken up into itself so much of the deepest religious experience of past generations.

C.H. Dodd

We have just enough religion to make us hate, but not enough to make us love one another.

Jonathan Swift

The devil can cite Scripture for his purpose.

William Shakespeare

The only really vital thing in religion is to become acquainted with God.

Hannah Whitall Smith

I have as much authority as the Pope – I just don't have as many people who believe it.

George Carlin

Christianity has not been tried and found wanting; it has been found difficult and not tried.

G.K. Chesterton

Religion is what keeps the poor from murdering the rich.

Napoleon Bonaparte

Every day people are straying away from the church and going back to God.

Lenny Bruce

Heaven and Hell

Heaven for climate;
hell for society.

Mark Twain

They say that hell is hot, but is it humid? Because I can take the heat; it's the humidity I can't stand.

Ronnie Shakes

Heaven, hell, the worlds are within us.
Man is the great abyss.

Henri Frédéric Amiel

The Catholic idea of heaven and hell is full of extremes. It's either eternal bliss, walking around on clouds playing table tennis with Mozart and Cary Grant, or eternal damnation where you have to light Hitler's cigars.

Paul Merton

I will spend my heaven doing good on Earth.

St Teresa

I shall be happy in heaven provided the angels are beautifully attired and wear their halos at a tilt.

Yves Saint Laurent

The safest road to hell is the gradual one – the gentle slope, soft underfoot, without sudden turnings, without milestones, without signposts.

C.S. Lewis

To love is to receive a glimpse of heaven.

Karen Sunde

Here there is no hope, and consequently no duty, no work, nothing to be gained by praying, nothing to be lost by doing what you like. Hell, in short, is a place where you have nothing to do but amuse yourself.

George Bernard Shaw

I believe that I am in hell, therefore I am there.

Arthur Rimbaud

A man's reach should exceed his grasp
– or what's a heaven for?

Robert Browning

In heaven an angel is
nobody in particular.
George Bernard Shaw

To see a world in a grain of sand
And a heaven in a wild flower,
Hold infinity in the palm of your hand
And eternity in an hour.

William Blake

My idea of heaven is eating *pâté de foie gras* to the
sound of trumpets

Sydney Smith

Hell is other people.

Jean-Paul Sartre

The human mind is inspired enough when it comes to
inventing horrors; it is when it tries to invent a heaven
that it shows itself cloddish.

Evelyn Waugh

In my Father's house are many mansions: if it were not so,
I would have told you. I go to prepare a place for you.

The Bible (Gospel of John)

I would renounce, therefore, the attempt to create heaven
on earth, and focus instead on reducing the hell.

A. Alan Borovoy

For mortal me there is but one hell, and that is the folly
and wickedness and spite of his fellows; but once his life is
over, there's an end to it: his annihilation is final and entire,
of him nothing survives.

Marquis de Sade

My soul can find no staircase to Heaven unless it be
through Earth's loveliness.

Michelangelo

I don't want to express an opinion. You see, I have
friends in both places.

Mark Twain

Visions of God

I do not feel obliged to believe that the same God who has endowed us with sense, reason, and intellect has intended us to forgo their use.

Galileo

He who leaveth home in search of knowledge walketh in the path of God.

Muhammad

This only is denied to God: the power to undo the past.

Agathon

Imagine the Creator as a stand-up comedian – and at once the world becomes explicable.

H.L. Mencken

The remarkable thing about the way in which people talk about God is that it seems to escape them completely that God hears what they are saying.

Søren Kierkegaard

The atheist who is moved by love is moved by the spirit of God; an atheist who lives by love is saved by his faith in God whose existence (under that name) he denies.

William Temple

God is a comedian playing to an audience too afraid to laugh.

Voltaire

If it turns out that there is a God, I don't think that he's evil. But the worst that you can say about him is that basically he's an underachiever.

Woody Allen

When men cease to believe in God, they will not believe in nothing, they will believe in anything.

G.K. Chesterton

I would rather live my life as if there is a God and die to find out there isn't, than live my life as if there isn't and die to find out there is.

Albert Camus

God moves in a mysterious way,
His wonders to perform.

William Cowper

The creator of the universe works in mysterious ways.
But he uses a base ten counting system and likes round numbers.

Scott Adams

If there were no God, there would be no atheists.

G.K. Chesterton

God is not a cosmic bellboy for whom we can press a button to get things done.

Harry Emerson Fosdick

I've been hiding from God, and I'm appalled to find how easy it is.

Mignon McLaughlin

My dear child, you must believe in God in spite of what the clergy tell you.

Benjamin Jowett

If God did not exist, it would be necessary to invent him.
Voltaire

I am still an atheist, thank God.
Luis Buñuel

God, whatever else He is – and of course He is everything else – is not a fool.

Alan Bennett

An atheist is a man who has no invisible means of support.
John Buchan

God is the Being that may properly only be addressed, not expressed.

Martin Buber

I know I am God because when I pray to him I find I'm talking to myself.

Peter Barnes

Man created God in his image.
Bertrand Russell

Quotations
for **funerals** and **memorials**

When a friend or loved one dies, well-chosen words can bring solace, evoke happy memories and help to bridge the emotional gap. Whether you want to celebrate a treasured life, or simply look for comfort, a thoughtful quotation can ease the loss.

One always dies too soon – or too late. And yet one's whole life is complete at that moment, with a line drawn neatly under it, ready for the summing up.

Jean-Paul Sartre

Do not stand at my grave and weep.
I am not there, I do not sleep.
I am the thousand winds that blow.
I am diamond glints on snow.
I am the sunlight on ripened grain.
I am gentle autumnal rain.
When you waken in the morning hush.
I am the soft uplifting rush
Of quiet birds in circled flight.
I am the soft stars that shine at night.
Do not stand at my grave and cry –
I am not there. I did not die.

Anon

Man that is born of a woman hath but a short time to live, and is full of misery. He cometh up, and is cut down, like a flower; he fleeth as it were a shadow, and never continueth in one stay.

The Book of Common Prayer

The dead don't die. They look on and help.

D.H. Lawrence

The event of death is always astounding; our philosophy never reaches, never possesses it; we are always at the beginning of our catechism; always the definition is yet to be made. What is death?

Ralph Waldo Emerson

Death is a challenge. It tells us not to waste time. It tells us to tell each other right now that we love each other.

Leo Buscaglia

As a well-spent day brings happy sleep, so a life well spent brings happy death.

Leonardo da Vinci

O death, where is thy sting?
O grave, where is thy
victory?

The Bible (I Corinthians)

For a season, there must be pain –
For a little, little space
I shall lose the sight of her face,
Take back the old life again
While She is at rest in her place.

Rudyard Kipling

We die containing a richness of lovers and
tribes, tastes we have swallowed, bodies we
have plunged into and swum up as if rivers of
wisdom, characters we have climbed into as if
trees, fears we have hidden as if in caves.

Michael Ondaatje

There is no cure for birth
and death save to enjoy the interval.

George Santayana

Blessed are they that mourn:
for they shall be comforted

The Bible (Gospel of Matthew)

Any man's death diminishes me, because I am
involved in Mankind; and therefore never send to
know for whom the bell tolls: it tolls for thee.

John Donne

It matters not how a
man dies, but how he
lives. The act of dying
is not of importance, it
lasts so short a time.

Samuel Johnson

As virtuous men pass mildly away,
And whisper to their souls to go,
Whilst some of their sad friends do say
'Now his breath goes,' and some say, 'No.'
So let us melt, and make no noise,
No tear-floods, nor sigh-tempests move;
'Twere profanation of our joys
To tell the laity our love.

John Donne

Death is nothing at all. It does not count. I
have only slipped away into the next room.
Nothing has happened. Everything remains
exactly as it was. I am I, and you are you, and
the old life that we lived so fondly together is
untouched, unchanged … There is absolute
and unbroken continuity. What is this death
but a negligible accident? Why should I be
out of mind because I am out of sight? I am but
waiting for you, for an interval, somewhere
very near, just around the corner.

Henry Scott Holland

Knowledge and learning

> You live and learn. At any rate, you live.
>
> **Douglas Adams**

The illiterate of the 21st century will not be those who cannot read and write, but those who cannot learn, unlearn and relearn.

Alvin Toffler

You can never learn less, you can only learn more.

R. Buckminster Fuller

New knowledge is the most valuable commodity on earth. The more truth we have to work with, the richer we become.

Kurt Vonnegut

You ain't learnin' nothin' when you're talkin'.

Lyndon B. Johnson

I was born not knowing and have had only a little time to change that here and there.

Richard P. Feynman

Learning is not compulsory ... neither is survival.

W. Edwards Deming

The immature mind hops from one thing to another; the mature mind seeks to follow through.

Harry A. Overstreet

We now accept the fact that learning is a lifelong process of keeping abreast of change. And the most pressing task is to teach people how to learn.

Peter F. Drucker

I find that a great part of the information I have was acquired by looking up something and finding something else on the way.

Franklin P. Adams

A sense of curiosity is nature's original school of education.

Smiley Blanton

What is important is to keep learning, to enjoy challenge, and to tolerate ambiguity. In the end there are no certain answers.

Martina Horner

Learn as much by writing as by reading.

Lord Acton

Try to learn something about everything and everything about something.

Thomas H. Huxley

If little else, the brain is an educational toy.

Tom Robbins

Nothing that you will learn in the course of your studies will be of the slightest possible use to you in after life – save only this – that if you work hard and intelligently you should be able to detect when a man is talking rot, and that, in my view, is the main, if not the sole, purpose of education.

J.A. Smith

Scepticism: the mark and even the pose of the educated mind.

John Dewey

I have tried to know absolutely nothing about a great many things, and I have succeeded fairly well.

Robert Benchley

> Those people who think they know everything are a great annoyance to those of us who do.
> **Isaac Asimov**

It is a miracle that curiosity survives formal education.

Albert Einstein

We don't know a millionth of one percent about anything.

Thomas Alva Edison

It is the mark of an educated mind to be able to entertain a thought without accepting it.

Aristotle

Just think of the tragedy of teaching children not to doubt.

Clarence Darrow

A little learning is a dangerous thing;
Drink deep, or taste not the Pierian spring.

Alexander Pope

Words of wisdom

Better be wise by the misfortunes of others than by your own.

Aesop

As a human being, one has been endowed with just enough intelligence to be able to see clearly how utterly inadequate that intelligence is when confronted with what exists.

Albert Einstein

Everyone is wise until he speaks.

Irish proverb

If one is too lazy to think, too vain to do a thing badly, too cowardly to admit it, one will never attain wisdom.

Cyril Connolly

The days that make us happy make us wise.

John Masefield

Cleverness and stupidity are generally in the same boat against wisdom.

J.A. Spender

Growth in wisdom may be exactly measured by decrease in bitterness.

Friedrich Nietzsche

The next best thing to being wise oneself is to live in a circle of those who are.

C.S. Lewis

It's so simple to be wise. Just think of something stupid to say, and then don't say it.

Sam Levenson

Wisdom doesn't necessarily come with age. Sometimes age shows up all by itself.

Tom Wilson

Wisdom comes from experience. Experience is often a result of lack of wisdom.

Terry Pratchett

God, grant me the serenity to accept the things I cannot change, the courage to change the things I can, and the wisdom to know the difference.

Reinhold Niebuhr

It is a profitable thing, if one is wise, to seem foolish.

Aeschylus

You can tell whether a man is clever by his answers. You can tell whether a man is wise by his questions.

Naguib Mahfouz

It requires wisdom to understand wisdom: the music is nothing if the audience is deaf.

Walter Lippmann

If 50 million people say a foolish thing, it is still a foolish thing.

Anatole France

Wisdom consists of the anticipation of consequences.

Norman Cousins

Wisdom is the quality that keeps you from getting into situations where you need it.

Doug Larson

The wisest mind has something yet to learn.

George Santayana

Cleverness is not wisdom.
Euripides

The art of **being wise** is the art of **knowing** what to overlook.

William James

The fool wonders, the wise man asks.
Benjamin Disraeli

Mix a little foolishness with your prudence: It's good to be silly at the right moment.

Horace

Intelligence is quickness to apprehend as distinct from ability, which is capacity to act wisely on the thing apprehended.

Alfred North Whitehead

Nothing but the truth

It is always a sign of mediocrity in people when they flock together; only individuals seek the truth.

Boris Pasternak

The truth does not change according to our ability to stomach it.

Flannery O'Connor

Chase after truth like hell and you'll free yourself, even though you never touch its coat-tails.

Clarence Darrow

Believe those who are seeking the truth; doubt those who find it.

André Gide

Truth is what stands the test of experience.

Albert Einstein

When I tell the truth, it is not for the sake of convincing those who do not know it, but for the sake of defending those that do.

William Blake

Truth sits upon the lips of dying men.

Matthew Arnold

Truth emerges more readily from error than from confusion.

Francis Bacon

Like all virtuous people, he imagines he must speak the truth.

Joyce Carol Oates

Everything you can imagine is real.

Pablo Picasso

Truth is so rare that it is delightful to tell it.

Emily Dickinson

Never assume the obvious is true.

William Safire

I have a theory that the truth is never told during the nine-to-five hours.

Hunter S. Thompson

There are two kinds of truth: the truth that lights the way, and the truth that warms the heart. The first of these is science, and the second is art.

Raymond Chandler

We don't see things as they are, we see them as we are.

Anaïs Nin

The minute one utters a certainty, the opposite comes to mind.

May Sarton

Anything could be true or false, depending on whether one believed it.

Laura Esquivel

All generalisations are dangerous, even this one.
Alexandre Dumas

Say not, 'I have found the truth', but rather, 'I have found a truth'.

Kahlil Gibran

Bad taste is simply saying the truth before it should be said.

Mel Brooks

There are few nudities so objectionable as the naked truth.

Agnes Repplier

'Tis strange – but true; for truth is always strange; Stranger than fiction.

Lord Byron

It is one thing to show a man that he is in error, and another to put him in possession of truth.

John Locke

Respect for the truth comes close to being the basis for all morality.

Frank Herbert

Truth, when witty, is the wittiest of all things.

Julius and Augustus Hare

The meaning of life

> The main thing is to keep the main thing the main thing.
> **Stephen Covey**

Of course life has no point. If it had man would not be free, he'd become a slave to that point and his life would be governed by completely new criteria: the criteria of slavery.
Andrei Tarkovsky

I feel that life is divided up into the horrible and the miserable.
Woody Allen

Here is the test to find whether your mission on earth is finished: if you're alive, it isn't.
Richard Bach

Life and love are life and love, a bunch of violets is a bunch of violets, and to drag in the idea of a point is to ruin everything. Live and let live, love and let love, flower and fade, and follow the natural curve, which flows on, pointless.
D.H. Lawrence

Life is something to do when you can't get to sleep.
Fran Lebowitz

As far as we can discern, the sole purpose of human existence is to kindle a light in the darkness of mere being.
Carl Jung

Life is an onion which one peels crying.
French proverb

Life is without meaning. You bring the meaning to it. The meaning of life is whatever you ascribe it to be. Being alive is the meaning.
Joseph Campbell

Life has its own hidden forces which you can only discover by living.
P.R. Régamey

We are here to add what we can to life, not to get what we can from it.

William Osler

People want to find a 'meaning' in everything and everyone. That's the disease of our age – an age that is anything but practical but believes itself to be more practical than any other age.
Pablo Picasso

I don't want to get to the end of my life and find that
I lived just the length of it. I want to have lived the width
of it as well.

Diane Ackerman

It is not peace we seek but meaning.

Lawrence Durrell

Happy the man, and happy he alone,
He, who can call today his own:
He who, secure within, can say,
Tomorrow do thy worst, for I have lived today.

John Dryden

Our whole life is spent in sketching an ineradicable
portrait of ourselves.

André Gide

The main things which seem to me important on their
own account, and not merely as means to other things,
are knowledge, art, instinctive happiness, and relations
of friendship or affection.

Bertrand Russell

When I discover who I am, I'll be free.

Ralph Ellison

Life is just one damned thing after another.

Elbert Hubbard

We're here for a reason. I believe a bit of the reason is to
throw little torches out to lead people through the dark.

Whoopi Goldberg

> There are two ways to
> live: you can live as if
> nothing is a miracle;
> you can live as if
> everything is a miracle.
> **Albert Einstein**

*The answer to
the great question
of Life, the
Universe and
Everything is ...
forty-two.*

Douglas Adams

KARL MARX

SIGMUND FREUD

MOTHER TERESA

RICHARD BRANSON

F. SCOTT FITZGERALD

ERNEST HEMINGWAY

P.G.

CHARLES DE GAULLE

W. SOMERSET MAUGHAM

PETER USTINOV

MICHELANGELO

EDDIE IZZARD

ALBERT CAMUS

ALAN BENNETT

GEORGE BERNARD

JOAN RIVERS

JONATHAN SWIFT

QUENTIN CRISP

W.H. AUDEN

MUHAMMAD ALI

DOLLY PARTON

JEAN-PAUL SARTRE

GEORGE ORWELL

WALT DISNEY

DOUGLAS ADAMS

JOHN F. KENNEDY

DOROTHY PARKER

ALBERT EINSTEIN

FRANK ZAPPA

NELSON MANDELA

OSCAR WILDE

MARGARET THATCHER

PABLO PICASSO AESOP

MARK TWAIN

LEO TOLSTOY

ORSON WELLES

ISAAC ASIMOV

WODEHOUSE BILL CLINTON

BUDDHA GROUCHO MARX

VIRGINIA WOOLF

JANE AUSTEN SAMUEL PEPYS

W.C. FIELDS MARILYN MONROE

SHAW

PLEASURES
AND PASTIMES

Sit back and relax

I have had a holiday, and I'd like to take it up professionally.

Kylie Minogue

We should rest and amuse ourselves in such a way that rest and amusement do not become an additional fatigue or a total waste of time.

Alexis Carrel

To work is simple enough; but to rest, there is the difficulty.

Ernest Hello

I find I haven't the art of rest … Probably the great workers of the world have been the great masters of the art of resting.

Stephen MacKenna

To be able to fill leisure intelligently is the last product of civilisation, and at present very few people have reached this level.

Bertrand Russell

I go to bed early. My favourite dream comes on at nine.

Eddie Izzard

To sit in the shade on a fine day, and look upon verdure is the most perfect refreshment.

Jane Austen

There must be quite a few things a hot bath won't cure, but I don't know many of them.

Sylvia Plath

Far from idleness being the root of all evil, it is rather the only true good.

Søren Kierkegaard

Lying in bed would be an altogether perfect and supreme experience if only one had a coloured pencil long enough to draw on the ceiling.

G.K. Chesterton

People seem to enjoy things more when they know a lot of other people have been left out of the pleasure.

Russell Baker

You have to allow a certain amount of time in which you
are doing nothing in order to have things occur to you,
to let your mind think.

Mortimer J. Adler

One of the most adventurous things left us is to go to bed.
For no one can lay a hand on our dreams.

E.V. Lucas

Arranging a bowl of flowers in the morning can give
a sense of quiet in a crowded day – like writing a poem,
or saying a prayer.

Anne Morrow Lindbergh

Spend the afternoon. You can't take it with you.

Annie Dillard

Good friends, good books and a sleepy conscience:
this is the ideal life.

Mark Twain

If you can spend a perfectly
useless afternoon in a perfectly
useless manner, you have
learned how to live.

Lin Yutang

It's all right letting yourself go as
long as you can let yourself back.

Mick Jagger

No man needs a vacation so much
as the man who has just had one.

Elbert Hubbard

There is no pleasure in having nothing
to do; the fun is in having lots to do and not doing it.

Mary Wilson Little

Time you enjoy wasting was not wasted.

John Lennon

It is in his pleasure that a man really lives; it is from his
leisure that he constructs the true fabric of self.

Agnes Repplier

It was such a lovely
day, I thought it a
pity to get up.

W. Somerset Maugham

I want to be alone

> We live, as we dream, alone.
>
> **Joseph Conrad**

Solitude is a wonderful thing when one is at peace with oneself and when there is a definite task to be accomplished.

Johann Wolfgang von Goethe

I love to be alone. I never found the companion that was so companionable as solitude.

Henry David Thoreau

To calm your mind, go for a walk at dawn in the park, or watch the dew on a rose in the garden. Lie on the ground and gaze up into the sky. Let the sky outside awake a sky inside your mind.

Sogyal Rinpoche

The Lord had the wonderful advantage of being able to work alone.

Kofi Annan

When I got to school, I ran away again in desperation for my ration of solitude. I'm nullified without it. Like water from a creek to a vagabond, it is necessary to me.

Sylvia Ashton-Warner

In solitude, where we are least alone.

Lord Byron

Language has created the word 'loneliness' to express the pain of being alone. And it has created the word 'solitude' to express the glory of being alone.

Paul Tillich

I never said, 'I want to be alone.' I only said, 'I want to be left alone.' There is all the difference.

Greta Garbo

Loneliness is and always has been the central and inevitable experience of every man.

Thomas Wolfe

The mark of solitude is silence, as speech is the mark of community. Silence and speech have the same inner correspondence and difference as do solitude and community. One does not exist without the other. Right speech comes out of silence, and right silence comes out of speech.

Dietrich Bonhoeffer

I hold this to be the highest task for a bond between two people: that each protects the solitude of the other.

Rainer Maria Rilke

Solitude, though it may be silent as light, is like light, the mightiest of agencies; for solitude is essential to man. All men come into this world alone and leave it alone.

Thomas de Quincey

It's a rather pleasant experience to be alone in a bank at night.

Willie Sutton

I feel the same way about solitude as some people feel about the blessing of the church. It's the light of grace for me. I never close my door behind me without the awareness that I am carrying out an act of mercy toward myself.

Peter Hoeg

You cannot be lonely if you like the person you're alone with.

Wayne Dyer

The whole value of solitude depends upon one's self; it may be a sanctuary or a prison, a haven of repose or a place of punishment, a heaven or a hell, as we ourselves make it.

John Lubbock

He who does not enjoy solitude will not love freedom.

Arthur Schopenhauer

Solitude is a world in itself, full of wonders and resources unthought of. It is absurdly near; yet so unapproachably distant.

Rabindranath Tagore

The person who does not enjoy his own company is usually right.
Coco Chanel

We're all of us sentenced to solitary confinement inside our own skins.
Tennessee Williams

Be my guest

Santa Claus has the right idea; visit people once a year.

Victor Borge

His shortcoming
is his long staying.

Benjamin Disraeli

At a dinner party one should eat wisely but not too well, and talk well but not too wisely.

W. Somerset Maugham

In England people actually try to be brilliant at breakfast. That is so dreadful of them! Only dull people are brilliant at breakfast.

Oscar Wilde

A crust eaten in peace is better than a banquet partaken in anxiety.

Aesop

The lintel low enough to keep out pomp and pride;
The threshold high enough to turn deceit aside;
The doorband strong enough from robbers to defend;
This door will open at a touch to welcome every friend.

Henry Jackson van Dyke

No matter how many chairs you provide, guests always sit on the edge of a little table and knock sherry on the carpet.

Paul Jennings

At every party there are two kinds of people – those who want to go home and those who don't. The trouble is, they are usually married to each other.

Ann Landers

The telephone is a good way to talk to people without having to offer them a drink.

Fran Lebowitz

Never give a party if you will be the most interesting person there.

Mickey Friedman

After all, what is your host's purpose in having a party? Surely not for you to enjoy yourself; if that were their sole purpose, they'd have simply sent champagne and women over to your place by taxi.

P.J. O'Rourke

Hospitality consists in a little fire, a little food, and an immense quiet.

Ralph Waldo Emerson

Like other parties of the kind, it was first silent, then talky, then argumentative, then disputatious, then unintelligible, then altogethery, then inarticulate, and then drunk.

Lord Byron

Some people can stay longer in an hour than others can in a week.

William Dean Howells

Fish and visitors stink after three days.

Benjamin Franklin

Some cause happiness wherever they go; others whenever they go.

Oscar Wilde

Whenever, at a party, I have been in the mood to study fools, I have always looked for a great beauty: they always gather round her like flies around a fruit stall.

Jean Paul Richter

It is equally offensive to speed a guest who would like to stay and to detain one who is anxious to leave.

Homer

A banquet is probably the most fatiguing thing in the world – except ditchdigging.

Mark Twain

The Life and Soul, the man who will never go home while there is one man, woman or glass of anything not yet drunk.

Katharine Whitehorn

Did you ever go to a party, go in the bathroom, flush the toilet, and the water starts coming up? That is the most frightening moment in the life of a human being.

Jerry Seinfeld

At the end of every party there is always a girl crying.
Peter Kay

Dinner parties are given mostly in the middle classes by way of revenge.

William Makepiece Thackeray

House and home

Cleaning your house while your kids are still growing is like shovelling the walk before it stops snowing.

Phyllis Diller

The first thing in one's home is comfort; let beauty of detail be added if one has the means, the patience, the eye.

George Gissing

One's own surroundings mean so much to one, when one is feeling miserable.

Edith Sitwell

Home is the only place where you can go out and in. There are places you can go into, and places you can go out of, but one place, if you do but find it, where you go out and in both, is home.

George Macdonald

Have nothing in your house that you do not know to be useful, or believe to be beautiful.

William Morris

Of all hateful occupations, housekeeping is to my mind the most hateful.

Hannah Whitall Smith

At the worst, a house unkept cannot be so distressing as a life unlived.

Rose Macaulay

There's no greater bliss in life than when the plumber eventually comes to unblock the drains. No writer can give that sort of pleasure.

Victoria Glendinning

Home life as we understand it is no more natural to us than a cage is to a cockatoo.

George Bernard Shaw

Space and light and order. Those are the things that men need just as much as they need bread or a place to sleep.

Le Corbusier

Home is the place where, when you have to go there, they have to take you in.

Robert Frost

May your walls know joy. May every room hold laughter and every window open to great possibility.

Mary Anne Radmacher

The poorest man may in his cottage bid defiance to all the forces of the Crown. It may be frail – its roof may shake – the wind may blow through it – the rain may enter – but the King of England cannot enter – all his force dares not cross the threshold of the ruined tenement!

William Pitt, the Elder

The home is the chief school of human virtues.

William Ellery Channing

Home is where you come to when you have nothing better to do.

Margaret Thatcher

A good home must be made, not bought.

Joyce Maynard

The happiness of the domestic fireside is the first boon of Heaven; and it is well it is so, since it is that which is the lot of the mass of mankind.

Thomas Jefferson

The ringing of a telephone is always louder in an empty house.

Joyce Carol Oates

My kitchen is a mystical place, a kind of temple for me. It is a place where the surfaces seem to have a significance, where the sounds and odours carry meaning that transfers from the past and bridges to the future.

Pearl Bailey

Home is where the mortgage is.

Billy Connolly

When you dwell in a house you dislike, you will look out of a window a deal more than those that are content with their dwelling.

Mary Webb

It is a most miserable thing to feel ashamed of home.

Charles Dickens

Housework expands to fill the time available, plus half an hour.

Shirley Conran

Quotations
for **celebrations**
and **birthdays**

The years may fly by, but anniversaries and birthdays are always a great excuse to pause for a celebration. Bringing some choice words to a gathering of friends and family can add laughter and fond reflection to the occasion.

An anniversary is a time to celebrate the joys of today, the memories of yesterday, and the hopes of tomorrow.

Anon

A wedding anniversary is the celebration of love, trust, partnership, tolerance and tenacity. The order varies for any given year.

Paul Sweeney

It is a sobering thought …
that when Mozart was my age
he had been dead for two years.

Tom Lehrer

I am just turning 40 and taking my time about it.
Harold Lloyd

Let us celebrate the occasion
with wine and sweet words.
Plautus

There is still
no cure for
the common
birthday.

John Glenn

You must have been warned against letting the golden hours slip by; but some of them are golden only because we let them slip by.

J.M. Barrie

When I was young, I was told: 'You'll see, when you're 50.' I am 50 and I haven't seen a thing.
Erik Satie

Three things happen when you get to my age. First your memory starts to go ... and I have forgotten the other two.
Denis Healey

Christmas! 'Tis the season for kindling the fire of hospitality in the hall, the genial fire of charity in the heart.
Washington Irving

You know you're getting old when you get that one candle on the cake. It's like, 'See if you can blow this out.'
Jerry Seinfeld

If I'd known I was gonna live this long, I'd have taken better care of myself.
Eubie Blake (on his 100th birthday)

I recently turned 60. Practically a third of my life is over.
Woody Allen

I am 46, and have been for some time past.
Anita Brookner

Christmas is a time when you get homesick – even when you're home.
Carol Nelson

Thirty-five is a very attractive age. London society is full of women of the very highest birth who have, of their own free choice, remained thirty-five for years.
Oscar Wilde

Ring out the old, ring in the new,
Ring, happy bells, across the snow:
The year is going, let him go;
Ring out the false, ring in the true.
Alfred, Lord Tennyson

Our wedding was many years ago. The celebration continues to this day.
Gene Perret

Food and cooking

Men like to barbecue. Men like to cook only if danger is involved.

Rita Rudner

What makes food such a tyranny for women? A man may in times of crisis hit the bottle, but he rarely hits the fridge.

Joanna Trollope

If you feel depressed or let down, my advice is to roast a chicken.

Delia Smith

I tell the kids they should throw away the cereal and eat the box. At least they'd get some fibre.

Dr Richard Holstein

I declare that a meal prepared by a person who loves you will do more good than any average cooking, and on the other side of it a person who dislikes you is bound to get that dislike into your food, without intending to.

Luther Burbank

I believe that if ever I had to practice cannibalism, I might manage if there were enough tarragon around.

James Beard

All happiness depends on a leisurely breakfast.

John Gunter

If slaughterhouses had glass walls, everyone would be a vegetarian.

Paul McCartney

Vegetarians are like animal rights protesters: they cannot just get on with their chosen, dreary approach to life. They have to scream at the rest of us as if this is going to bring us to our senses.

Janet Street-Porter

I was a vegetarian until I started leaning towards the sunlight.

Rita Rudner

My favourite animal is steak.

Fran Lebowitz

The most remarkable thing about my mother is that for 30 years she served the family nothing but leftovers. The original meal has never been found.

Calvin Trillin

It's odd how all men develop the notion, as they grow older, that their mothers were wonderful cooks. I have yet to meet a man who will admit that his mother was a kitchen assassin and nearly poisoned him.

Robertson Davies

What I say is that, if a man really likes potatoes, he must be a pretty decent sort of fellow.

A.A. Milne

My wife and I tried two or three times in the last 40 years to have breakfast together, but it was so disagreeable we had to stop.

Winston Churchill

Strange to see how a good dinner and feasting reconciles everybody.

Samuel Pepys

Sometimes … we want to feel not like a post-modern, post-feminist, overstretched modern woman but, rather, a domestic goddess, trailing nutmeggy fumes of baking pie in our languorous wake.

Nigella Lawson

Life is too short to stuff a mushroom.

Shirley Conran

Cooking is like love. It should be entered into with abandon or not at all.

Harriet van Horne

Tell me what you eat, and I will tell you what you are.

Anthelme Brillat-Savarin

My doctor told me to stop having intimate dinners for four. Unless there are three other people.

Orson Welles

> The French, they say, live to eat. The English, on the other hand, eat to die.
>
> **Martin Amis**

Everything I have I owe to spaghetti.

Sophia Loren

Wine and drinking

I'm only a beer teetotaller, not a champagne teetotaller.

George Bernard Shaw

Great people talk about ideas, average people talk about things, and small people talk about wine.

Fran Lebowitz

The wines that one remembers best are not necessarily the finest that one has tasted, and the highest quality may fail to delight so much as some far more humble beverage drunk in more favourable surroundings.

H. Warner Allen

The rapturous, wild, and ineffable pleasure
Of drinking at somebody else's expense.

Henry Sambrooke Leigh

Wine is a treacherous friend who you must always be on guard for.

Christian Nestell Bovee

Not all chemicals are bad. Without chemicals such as hydrogen and oxygen, for example, there would be no way to make water, a vital ingredient in beer.

Dave Barry

Love makes the world go round? Whisky makes it go round twice as fast.

Compton Mackenzie

One reason I don't drink is that I want to know when I am having a good time.

Nancy Astor

There are five stages of drunkenness: verbose, jocose, lachrymose, bellicose, comatose.

Jeffrey Bernard

Only Irish coffee provides in a single glass all four essential food groups: alcohol, caffeine, sugar and fat.

Alex Levine

Can't we just get rid of wine lists? Do we really have to be reminded every time we go out to a nice restaurant that we have no idea what we are doing? Why don't they just give us a trigonometry quiz with the menu?

Jerry Seinfeld

A bottle of wine begs to be shared; I have never met a miserly wine lover.

Clifton Fadiman

An alcoholic is a man you don't like who drinks as much as you do.

Dylan Thomas

A glass of good wine is a gracious creature, and reconciles poor mortality to itself, and that is what few things can do.

Walter Scott

English coffee tastes like water that has been squeezed out of a wet sleeve.

Fred Allen

It is difficult to enjoy a good wine in a bad glass.

Evelyn Waugh

Whatever you tell them, people always make your tea or coffee the way they like it.

Russell Bell

I'm not so think as you drunk I am.

J.C. Squire

A man who exposes himself when he is intoxicated, has not the art of getting drunk.

Samuel Johnson

Water is the only drink for a wise man.

Henry David Thoreau

I'm ombibulous. I drink every known alcoholic drink, and enjoy them all.

H.L. Mencken

I don't drink water. Have you seen the way it rusts pipes?

W.C. Fields

Humour and laughter

A little nonsense now and then is cherished by the wisest men.
Roald Dahl

Humour is also a way of saying something serious.

T.S. Eliot

Humour is perhaps a sense of intellectual perspective: an awareness that some things are really important, others not; and that the two kinds are most oddly jumbled in everyday affairs.

Christopher Morley

When a thing is funny, search it carefully for a hidden truth.

George Bernard Shaw

It is the ability to take a joke, not make one, that proves you have a sense of humour.

Max Eastman

Defining and analysing humour is a pastime of humourless people.

Robert Benchley

Mark my words, when a society has to resort to the lavatory for its humour, the writing is on the wall.

Alan Bennett

I think it's the duty of the comedian to find out where the line is drawn and cross it deliberately.

George Carlin

A caricature is putting the face of a joke on the body of a truth.

Joseph Conrad

Laughter is inner jogging.

Norman Cousins

Humour can be dissected, as a frog can, but the thing dies in the process.

E.B. White

Wit is educated insolence.

Aristotle

If I had no sense of humour, I should long ago have committed suicide.

Mahatma Gandhi

You cannot be mad at somebody who makes you laugh – it's as simple as that.

Jay Leno

Comedy is tragedy plus time.

Carol Burnett

It is characteristic of all deep human problems that they are not to be approached without some humour and some bewilderment.

Freeman Dyson

Humour is just another defence against the universe.

Mel Brooks

The aim of a joke is not to degrade the human being, but to remind him that he is already degraded.

George Orwell

That is the saving grace of humour – if you fail, no one is laughing at you.

A. Whitney Brown

Those who don't know how to weep with their whole heart, don't know how to laugh either.

Golda Meir

A person without a sense of humour is like a wagon without springs. It's jolted by every pebble on the road.

Henry Ward Beecher

A sense of humour is just common sense, dancing.

Clive James

Men show their characters in nothing more clearly than in what they think laughable.

Johann Wolfgang von Goethe

Nobody ever died of laughter.

Max Beerbohm

Wit ought to be a glorious treat like caviar; never spread it about like marmalade.

Noël Coward

Talk talk

I'll not listen to reason ... Reason always means what someone else has got to say.

Elizabeth Gaskell

The real art of conversation is not only to say the right thing at the right place but to leave unsaid the wrong thing at the tempting moment.

Dorothy Nevill

One way to prevent conversation from being boring is to say the wrong thing.

Frank Sheed

My idea of an agreeable person is a person who agrees with me.

Benjamin Disraeli

The habit of common and continuous speech is a symptom of mental deficiency.

Walter Bagehot

Men of few words are the best men.

William Shakespeare

I have never been hurt by anything I didn't say.

Calvin Coolidge

Don't talk unless you can improve the silence.

Jorge Luis Borges

Show me someone who never gossips and I'll show you someone who isn't interested in people.

Barbara Walters

When people talk, listen completely. Most people never listen.

Ernest Hemingway

Many a secret that cannot be pried out by curiosity can be drawn out by indifference.

Sydney J. Harris

Too much agreement kills a chat.

Eldridge Cleaver

The present age is an age of talkers and not of doers;
and the reason is that the world is growing old.

William Hazlitt

People will accept your ideas much more readily if you tell
them Benjamin Franklin said it first.

David H. Comins

Charm is a way of getting the answer 'yes' without having
asked any clear question.

Albert Camus

When you say 'yes', say it quickly. But always take a half
hour to say no, so you can understand the other fellow's side.

Francis Cardinal Spellman

There are two things in ordinary conversation which
ordinary people dislike: information and wit.

Stephen Leacock

The boneless quality of English conversation, which,
so far as I have heard it, is all form and no content.

Margaret Halsey

Man invented language to satisfy his deep need to complain.
Lily Tomlin

A slip of the foot you
may soon recover, but a
slip of the tongue you
may never get over.
Benjamin Franklin

If you can't say anything good about
someone, sit right here by me.

Alice Roosevelt Longworth

There is no such thing as conversation. It is an illusion.
There are intersecting monologues, that is all.

Rebecca West

Gossip is when you hear something you like about
someone you don't.

Earl Wilson

They never taste who always drink;
They always talk, who never think.

Matthew Prior

Art for art's sake

> Art is anything you can get away with.
> **Marshall McLuhan**

There are only two styles of portrait painting: the serious and the smirk.

Charles Dickens

I don't know what art is, but I do know what it isn't. And it isn't someone walking around with a salmon over his shoulder, or embroidering the name of everyone they have slept with on the inside of a tent.

Brian Sewell

I'm a terrible cook, but if I could cook, I would see that as art as well; it's how much creative energy you put into something.

Tracy Emin

Abstract art: a product of the untalented sold by the unprincipled to the utterly bewildered.

Al Capp

There is no abstract art. You must always start with something. Afterward you can remove all traces of reality.

Pablo Picasso

The artist is nothing without the gift, but the gift is nothing without work.

Emile Zola

I always ask the sitter if they want truth or flattery. They always ask for truth, and I always give them flattery.

Ruskin Spear

If you want art to be like Ovaltine, then clearly some art is not for you.

Peter Reading

All the arts we practice are apprenticeship. The big art is our life.

M.C. Richards

The Holy Grail is to spend less time making the picture than it takes people to look at it.

Banksy

Art is made to disturb. Science reassures. There is only one valuable thing in art: the thing you cannot explain.

Georges Braque

Artists can colour the sky red because they know it's blue. Those of us who aren't artists must colour things the way they really are or people might think we're stupid.

Jules Feiffer

The only time I feel alive is when I'm painting.

Vincent Van Gogh

If a scientist were to cut his ear off, no one would take it as evidence of a heightened sensibility.

P.B. Medawar

Art is not a mirror but a hammer.

John Grierson

Art is a collaboration between God and the artist, and the less the artist does the better.

André Gide

If you have a burning restless urge to paint, simply eat something sweet and the feeling will pass.

Fran Lebowitz

The artist must be in his work as God is in creation, invisible and all-powerful; one must sense him everywhere but never see him.

Gustave Flaubert

Art is making something out of nothing and selling it.

Frank Zappa

Modern art is what happens when painters stop looking at girls and persuade themselves that they have a better idea.

John Ciardi

Art is either plagiarism or revolution.

Paul Gauguin

The adjective 'modern', when applied to any branch of art, means 'designed to evoke incomprehension, anger, boredom or laughter'.

Philip Larkin

Every time I paint a portrait I lose a friend.

John Singer Sargent

I saw the angel in the marble and I carved until I set him free.

Michelangelo

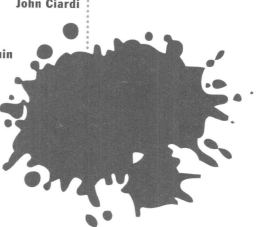

The silver screen

Hollywood is a place where people from Iowa mistake each other for stars.

Fred Allen

I think most of the people involved in any art always secretly wonder whether they are really there because they're good or there because they're lucky.

Katharine Hepburn

There are a thousand ways to point a camera, but really only one.

Ernst Lubitsch

We have our factory, which is called a stage. We make a product, we colour it, we title it and we ship it out in cans.

Cary Grant

Hollywood isn't anything like Hollywood.

Will Smith

Film is one of the three universal languages, the other two: mathematics and music.

Frank Capra

If my films make one more person miserable, I'll feel I have done my job.

Woody Allen

All American films boil down to 'I love you, Dad …'.

Ian Hislop

Never share a foxhole with a character who carries a photo of his sweetheart.

Del Close

The length of a film should be directly related to the endurance of the human bladder.

Alfred Hitchcock

Hollywood is a place where they'll pay you a thousand dollars for a kiss and fifty cents for your soul.

Marilyn Monroe

Stars are people who sell a lot of popcorn.

Harrison Ford

If you have to have a job in this world, a high-priced movie star is a pretty good gig.

Tom Hanks

Behind the phoney tinsel of Hollywood lies the real tinsel.

Oscar Levant

There are only six basic plots. *Frankenstein* and *My Fair Lady* are really the same story.

William Holden

Many actors want to play Hamlet and Macbeth, and ever since I became an actor from the very beginning, I just wanted to play a Shetland pony. I can't explain why.

Dustin Hoffman

American cinema is international like the fairy tales were international.

Bernard Tavernier

Acting is like a Halloween mask that you put on.

River Phoenix

A cult film is a movie that is seen about 50 times by about that many people.

Rick Bayan

One of the joys of going to the movies was that it was trashy, and we should never lose that.

Oliver Stone

Movie stars and monogamy go together like cornflakes and Tabasco.

Julia Llewellyn Smith

Why should people go out and pay to see bad movies when they can stay at home and see bad television for nothing?

Sam Goldwyn

Cinema is the most beautiful fraud in the world.
Jean-Luc Godard

A director must be a policeman, a midwife, a psychoanalyst, a sycophant and a bastard.

Billy Wilder

Woody Allen

MAKING ANGST AN ART FORM

From an early age, Brooklyn-born Woody Allen started to hone his art. As a teenage schoolboy in the early 1950s he wrote 50 jokes a day, and sold many of them to established comedians such as Sid Caesar, and talk show hosts Johnny Carson and Ed Sullivan. In the 1960s he worked as a stand-up comedian, sold short stories to *The New Yorker* magazine and began writing plays.

One of those plays, *Play It Again, Sam*, was made into a film in 1972, and it is film that has dominated Allen's creative life ever since, as actor, writer and director, all helping to confirm his comic genius. He has starred in many of his own movies, tending to play a character who is barely distinguishable from Allen in real life: neurotic, oppressed by sexual and existential angst, but at the same time brilliantly witty and articulate. Many of Allen's best and most quoted lines are fragments of dialogue delivered by his on-screen self.

Essentially, Woody Allen's gift is to make sparkling comedy out of the hopelessness of the human condition. His films and his writing are full of profoundly pithy gags and one-liners that, taken together, are like watching Jean-Paul Sartre do stand-up. He is, in the end, deadly serious. 'Life is full of misery, loneliness and suffering,' he has said, 'and it's all over much too soon.' You laugh, and then suddenly you stop laughing – because you realise it is all too true.

✳

A relationship, I think, is like a shark, you know? It has
to constantly move forward or it dies. And I think what
we got on our hands is a dead shark.

✳

Eighty per cent of success is showing up.

✳

It seemed the world was divided into good and bad people.
The good ones slept better … while the bad ones seemed
to enjoy the waking hours much more.

✳

I don't want to achieve immortality through my work.
I want to achieve it through not dying.

✳

I took a speed-reading course and read *War and Peace*
in 20 minutes. It involves Russia.

✳

If you're not failing every now and again, it's a sign
you're not doing anything very innovative.

✳

Love is the answer, but while you're waiting for the answer,
sex raises some pretty interesting questions.

✳

Time is nature's way of keeping everything from happening at once.

✳

94.5 per cent of all statistics are made up.

✳

I am a man who can't function well in life, but I can in art.

✳

Why are our days numbered and not, say, lettered?

On stage

All the world's a stage,
And all the men and women merely players;
They have their exits and their entrances;
And one man in his time plays many parts ...

William Shakespeare

> All the world's
> a stage and most
> of us are desperately
> unrehearsed.
>
> **Sean O'Casey**

If all the world's a stage, I want to operate the trapdoor.

Paul Beatty

The remarkable thing about Shakespeare is that he really is very good, in spite of all the people who say he is very good.

Robert Graves

There's nothing worse than actors who give the impression that they've taken on the priesthood. Acting is really about lying and, in my case, drinking coffee.

Johnny Depp

An actress can only play a woman. I'm an actor, I can play anything.

Whoopi Goldberg

Every actor in his heart believes everything bad that's printed about him.

Orson Welles

I really don't know who I am. Quite possibly, I do not exist at all.

Alec Guinness

To be a good actor you have to be something like a criminal, to be willing to break the rules to strive for something new.

Nicolas Cage

The play was a great success, but the audience was a disaster.

Oscar Wilde

Acting is like sex. You should do it, not talk about it.

Joanne Woodward

I think onstage nudity is disgusting, shameful and damaging to all things American. But if I were 22 with a great body, it would be artistic, tasteful, patriotic and a progressive religious experience.

Shelley Winters

Acting is a masochistic form of exhibitionism. It is not quite the occupation of an adult.

Laurence Olivier

Acting is not the things you say; it's the things you don't say.

Judi Dench

If I ever start talking about 'my craft' or 'my instrument', you have permission to shoot me point-blank.

Drew Barrymore

Actors never retire. They're just offered less and less work.

David Niven

The structure of a play is always the story of how the birds come home to roost.

Arthur Miller

I pretty much try to stay in a constant state of confusion – just because of the expression it leaves on my face.

Johnny Depp

Most of my nightmares involve me forgetting my lines in a stage play.

Robert Englund

There are two types: toupee actors and non-toupee actors.

Donald Pleasence

Acting is merely the art of keeping a large group of people from coughing.

Ralph Richardson

On the stage he was natural, simple, affecting; 'Twas only that when he was off he was acting.

Oliver Goldsmith

Critics are like eunuchs in a harem; they know how it's done, they've seen it done every day, but they're unable to do it themselves.

Brendan Behan

Character actress: an actress too ugly to be called a leading lady.

Kathy Burke

The **soundtrack** of your life

Music is spiritual. The music business is not.

Van Morrison

If music be the food of love, play on;
Give me excess of it, that surfeiting,
The appetite may sicken, and so die.

William Shakespeare

Canned music is like audible wallpaper.

Alistair Cooke

I have never thought of writing for reputation and honour.
What I have in my heart must come out; that is the reason
why I compose.

Ludwig van Beethoven

I love Beethoven, especially his poems.

Ringo Starr

Music hath charms to soothe a savage breast, to soften
rocks, or bend a knotted oak.

William Congreve

Music is the soundtrack of your life.
Dick Clark

Talking about music is like
dancing about architecture.
Steve Martin

Music is the art which is most
nigh to tears and memory.
Oscar Wilde

I only got seventh-grade
education, but I have a
doctorate in funk, and I like
to put that to good use.
James Brown

*All music is folk music, I ain't never
heard no horse sing a song.*

Louis Armstrong

Music is the only language in which
you cannot say a mean or sarcastic thing.

John Erskine

There's nothing remarkable about it. All one has to do is hit
the right keys at the right time and the instrument plays itself.

Johann Sebastian Bach

The notes I handle no better than many pianists. But the
pauses between the notes – ah, that is where the art resides!

Artur Schnabel

Music is well said to
be the speech of angels.

Thomas Carlyle

Music can be made anywhere, is
invisible and does not smell.

W.H. Auden

Every composer knows the anguish and despair occasioned
by forgetting ideas which one had no time to write down.

Hector Berlioz

Inspiration is wonderful when it happens, but the writer
must develop an approach for the rest of the time. The
wait is simply too long.

Leonard Bernstein

Music is your own experience, your thoughts, your wisdom.
If you don't live it, it won't come out of your horn.

Charlie Parker

You know what I hate about rock? I hate tie-dyed tee shirts.

Kurt Cobain

There are two golden rules for an orchestra: start together
and finish together. The public doesn't give a damn what
goes on in between.

Thomas Beecham

No opera plot can be sensible, for people do not sing
when they are feeling sensible.

W.H. Auden

A lot of pop music is
about stealing pocket
money for children.

Ian Anderson

Too many pieces of music finish too long after the end.

Igor Stravinsky

On the box

I don't watch television. I think it destroys the art of talking about oneself.

Stephen Fry

Anyone afraid of what he thinks television does to the world is probably just afraid of the world.

Clive James

I find television very educational. Whenever someone switches it on I go into another room and read a good book.

Groucho Marx

It is stupidvision – where most of the presenters look like they have to pretend to be stupid because they think their audience is. It patronises. It talks to the vacuum cleaner and the washing machine without much contact with the human brain.

Polly Toynbee

I hate television. I hate it as much as peanuts. But I can't stop eating peanuts.

Orson Welles

Television has made dictatorship impossible, but democracy unbearable.

Shimon Peres

Television is a medium of entertainment which permits millions of people to listen to the same joke at the same time, and yet remain lonesome.

T.S. Eliot

Let's face it, there are no plain women on television.

Anna Ford

Television contracts the imagination and radio expands it.

Terry Wogan

Television has proved that people will look at anything rather than each other.

Ann Landers

Every time you think television has hit its lowest ebb, a new programme comes along to make you wonder where you thought the ebb was.

Art Buchwald

A TV licence is a licence to print money.

Roy Thomson

Television thrives on unreason, and unreason thrives on television. It strikes at the emotions rather than the intellect.

Robin Day

Television is for appearing on, not looking at.

Noël Coward

Television was not invented to make human beings vacuous but is an emanation of their vacuity.

Malcolm Muggeridge

The word is half Greek, half Latin. No good can come of it.

C.P. Snow

Television is an invention that permits you to be entertained in your living room by people you wouldn't have in your home.

David Frost

Never miss a chance to have sex or appear on television.

Gore Vidal

The television, that insidious beast, that Medusa which freezes a billion people to stone every night, staring fixedly, that Siren which called and sang and promised so much and gave, after all, so little.

Ray Bradbury

Television is more interesting than people. If it were not, we should have people standing in the corners of our rooms.

Alan Coren

It is difficult to produce a television documentary that is both incisive and probing when every 12 minutes one is interrupted by 12 dancing rabbits singing about toilet paper.

Rod Serling

When television came roaring in after the war they did a little school survey asking children which they preferred and why – television or radio. And there was this seven-year-old boy who said he preferred radio 'because the pictures were better'.

Alistair Cooke

Television is actually closer to reality than anything in books. The madness of TV is the madness of human life.

Camille Paglia

The sporting life

> Some people think football is a matter of life and death. I assure you, it's much more serious than that.
>
> **Bill Shankly**

Every game ever invented by mankind is a way of making things hard for the fun of it.

John Ciardi

All I know most surely about morality and obligations, I owe to football.

Albert Camus

I tend to think that cricket is the greatest thing that God ever created on earth – certainly greater than sex, although sex isn't too bad either.

Harold Pinter

What do they know of cricket who only cricket know?

C.L.R. James

Power is only too happy to make football bear a diabolical responsibility for stupefying the masses.

Jean Baudrillard

Beyond the touchline there is nothing.

Jacques Derrida

Karate is a form of martial arts in which people who have had years and years of training can, using only their hands and feet, make some of the worst movies in the history of the world.

Dave Barry

In football everything is complicated by the presence of the opposing team.

Jean-Paul Sartre

Football is a game for rough girls, not suitable for delicate boys.

Oscar Wilde

Be bold. If you're going to make an error, make a doozy, and don't be afraid to hit the ball.

Billie Jean King

Golf is a good walk spoiled.

Mark Twain

Cricket to us was more than play, it was a worship in the summer sun.

Edmund Blunden

For when the One Great Scorer comes
To write against your name,
He marks – not that you won or lost –
But how you played the game.

Grantland Rice

The tactical difference between Association Football and Rugby with its varieties seems to be that in the former, the ball is the missile, in the latter, men are the missiles.

Alfred E. Crawley

There has never been a great athlete who died not knowing what pain is.

Bill Bradley

Champions aren't made in gyms. Champions are made from something they have deep inside them: a desire, a dream, a vision. The will must be stronger than the skill.

Muhammad Ali

We remember not the scores and the results in after years; it is the men who remain in our minds, in our imagination.

Neville Cardus

The essence of sports is that while you're doing it, nothing else matters, but after you stop, there is a place, generally not very important, where you would put it.

Roger Bannister

When you are not practicing, remember, someone somewhere is practicing, and when you meet him he will win.

Ed Macauley

I'm fanatical about sport: there seems to me something almost religious about the fact that human beings can organise play, the spirit of play.

Simon Gray

I play with a fear of letting people down. That's what motivates me.

Jonny Wilkinson

Baseball has the great advantage over cricket of being sooner ended.
George Bernard Shaw

Boxing is just show business with blood.
Frank Bruno

On the move

I don't hold with abroad, and think that foreigners speak English when our backs are turned.

Quentin Crisp

My favourite thing is to go where I've never been.

Diane Arbus

I wouldn't mind seeing China if I could come back the same day.

Philip Larkin

There is nothing like returning to a place that remains unchanged to find the ways in which you yourself have altered.

Nelson Mandela

Travel is only glamorous in retrospect.

Paul Theroux

No place is boring, if you've had a good night's sleep and have a pocket full of unexposed film.

Robert Adams

Remember, no matter where you go, there you are.

Earl Mac Rauch

If you don't know where you are going, any road will take you there.

Lewis Carroll

No changing of place at a hundred miles an hour ... will make us one whit stronger, happier or wiser. There was always more in the world than men could see, walked they ever so slowly; they will see it no better for going fast.

John Ruskin

What good is speed if the brain has oozed out on the way?

Karl Kraus

I am not a great cook, I am not a great artist, but I love art, and I love food, so I am the perfect traveller.

Michael Palin

At my age travel broadens the behind.

Stephen Fry

Not all who wander are lost.

J.R.R. Tolkien

Maps encourage boldness. They're like cryptic love letters. They make anything seem possible.

Mark Jenkins

Certainly, travel is more than the seeing of sights; it is a change that goes on, deep and permanent, in the ideas of living.

Miriam Beard

To travel hopefully is a better thing than to arrive.

Robert Louis Stevenson

Abroad is bloody.

King George VI

Wheresoever you go, go with all your heart.

Confucius

Everyone carries his own inch-rule of taste, and amuses himself by applying it, triumphantly, wherever he travels.

Henry Brooks Adams

The traveller sees what he sees, the tourist sees what he has come to see.

G.K. Chesterton

The worst thing about being a tourist is having other tourists recognise you as a tourist.

Russell Baker

Dorothy Parker

SHARPEST KNIFE IN THE BOX

She came to despise her reputation as queen of the wisecrack, and it is true that there was much more to Dorothy Parker than the clever one-liners that have ensured her fame. She was a perceptive observer of human weakness, and a sensitive poet. Some of her short lyrics are like frozen shards of emotion, as sharp and immediate as a snatched photograph.

But Parker will always be best remembered for her acid pen, sharpened in the New York magazine world, which she joined in her early 20s in 1916 with a job on *Vogue*. In her role as critic, most notably for *The New Yorker* magazine, she could nail mediocrity with a few steely words. She described *The House Beautiful* as 'the play lousy' and wrote (unfairly perhaps) that a performance by Katharine Hepburn 'runs the gamut of emotions from A to B'. Parker also had a nice line in Oscar Wilde-style paradoxes. She said, for example, that one should 'take care of the luxuries, and the necessities will take care of themselves'.

Quips like these made Parker sound shallow, but she was no such thing. She was a political radical, who reported on the Spanish Civil War, and a fierce advocate of civil rights. On her death in 1967, most of her estate went to Martin Luther King, Jnr, whom she greatly admired. The epitaph that she suggested for herself was 'Excuse my dust'.

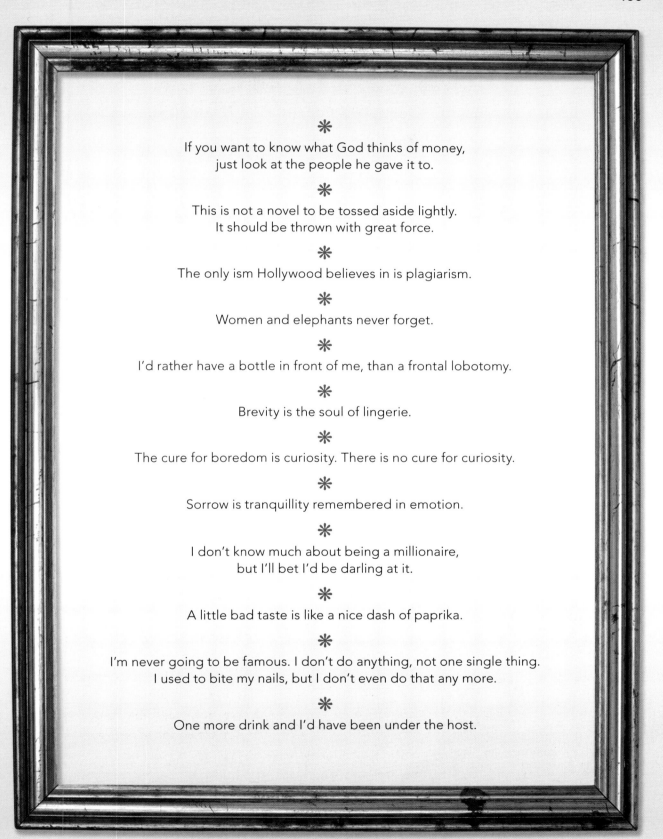

✳

If you want to know what God thinks of money,
just look at the people he gave it to.

✳

This is not a novel to be tossed aside lightly.
It should be thrown with great force.

✳

The only ism Hollywood believes in is plagiarism.

✳

Women and elephants never forget.

✳

I'd rather have a bottle in front of me, than a frontal lobotomy.

✳

Brevity is the soul of lingerie.

✳

The cure for boredom is curiosity. There is no cure for curiosity.

✳

Sorrow is tranquillity remembered in emotion.

✳

I don't know much about being a millionaire,
but I'll bet I'd be darling at it.

✳

A little bad taste is like a nice dash of paprika.

✳

I'm never going to be famous. I don't do anything, not one single thing.
I used to bite my nails, but I don't even do that any more.

✳

One more drink and I'd have been under the host.

Words and writing

Every journalist has a novel in him, which is an excellent place for it.

Russell Lynes

There are no limits to what you write as long as it increases the value of the paper you are writing on.

Buddy Ebsen

There have been a couple of books written about me by critics, but I don't read them because I don't want to know what my work is about.

Alan Bennett

Journal writing is a voyage to the interior.

Christina Baldwin

Self-knowledge does not necessarily help a novelist. It helps a human being a great deal, but novelists are often appalling human beings.

Peter Carey

Next to the writer of real estate advertisements, the autobiographer is the most suspect of prose artists.

Donal Henahan

I never read the life of any important person without discovering that he knew more and could do more than I could ever hope to know or to do in half a dozen lifetimes.

J.B. Priestley

'The Ancient Mariner' would not have taken so well if it had been called 'The Old Sailor'.

Samuel Butler

The reason why so few good books are written is that so few people who can write know anything.

Walter Bagehot

You never have to change anything you got up in the middle of the night to write.

Saul Bellow

Planning to write is not writing. Outlining, researching, talking to people about what you're doing, none of that is writing. Writing is writing.

E.L. Doctorow

Every great man nowadays has his disciples, and it is always Judas who writes the biography.

Oscar Wilde

A simile should be as exact as a slide-rule and as fresh as the smell of dill.

Isaak Babel

Love. Fall in love and stay in love. Write only what you love, and love what you write. The key word is love. You have to get up in the morning and write something you love, something to live for.

Ray Bradbury

All writing is a campaign against cliché.

Martin Amis

Novelists do not write as birds sing, by the push of nature. It is part of the job that there should be much routine and some daily stuff on the level of carpentry.

William Golding

The only reason for being a professional writer is that you can't help it.

Leo Rosten

Some editors are failed writers, but so are most writers.

T.S. Eliot

Literature is news that stays news.

Ezra Pound

There are three rules for writing a novel. Unfortunately, no one knows what they are.

W. Somerset Maugham

A poem is never finished, only abandoned.

Paul Valéry

What I like in a good author is not what he says but what he whispers.
Logan Pearsall Smith

For most of history, Anonymous was a woman.

Virginia Woolf

Books and reading

Never judge a book by its movie.
J.W. Egan

I gave up on new poetry myself 30 years ago, when most of it began to read like coded messages passing between lonely aliens on a hostile world.
Russell Baker

Reading is to the mind what exercise is to the body.
Joseph Addison

All books are either dreams or swords. You can cut, or you can drug, with words.
Amy Lowell

Man is what he reads.
Joseph Brodsky

Books are like lobster shells, we surround ourselves with 'em, then we grow out of 'em and leave 'em behind, as evidence of our earlier stages of development.
Dorothy L. Sayers

The covetous man who is in the extreme state of book-loving is the biblioklept, or book-stealer.
Andrew Lang

Wear the old coat and buy the new book.
Austin Phelps

There are worse crimes than burning books. One of them is not reading them.
Ray Bradbury

Reading is purloining another person's thoughts, instead of thinking with one's own head.
Arthur Schopenhauer

Hold a book in your hand and you're a pilgrim at the gates of a new city.
Anne Michaels

Always read stuff that will make you look good if you die in the middle of it.
P.J. O'Rourke

A best-seller is the gilded tomb of a mediocre talent.

Logan Pearsall Smith

In the case of good books, the point is not to see how many of them you can get through, but how many can get through to you.

Mortimer J. Adler

All good books have one thing in common – they are truer than if they had really happened.

Ernest Hemingway

Your borrowers of books – those mutilators of collections, spoilers of the symmetry of shelves, and creators of odd volumes.

Charles Lamb

There is no mistaking a real book when one meets it. It is like falling in love.

Christopher Morley

A book is a version of the world. If you do not like it, ignore it; or offer your own version in return.

Salman Rushdie

'What is the use of a book,' thought Alice, 'without pictures or conversations?'

Lewis Carroll

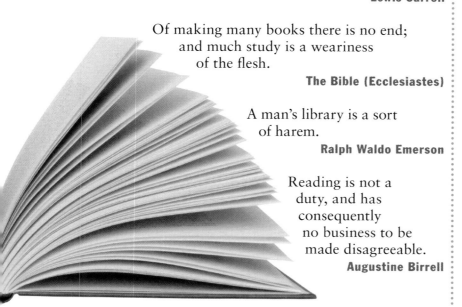

Of making many books there is no end; and much study is a weariness of the flesh.

The Bible (Ecclesiastes)

A man's library is a sort of harem.

Ralph Waldo Emerson

Reading is not a duty, and has consequently no business to be made disagreeable.

Augustine Birrell

KARL MARX

SIGMUND FREUD

MOTHER TERESA

RICHARD BRANSON

F. SCOTT FITZGERALD

ERNEST HEMINGWAY

P.G.

CHARLES DE GAULLE

W. SOMERSET MAUGHAM

PETER USTINOV

MICHELANGELO

EDDIE IZZARD

ALBERT CAMUS

ALAN BENNETT

GEORGE BERNARD

JOAN RIVERS

JONATHAN SWIFT

QUENTIN CRISP

W.H. AUDEN

MUHAMMAD ALI

DOLLY PARTON

JEAN-PAUL SARTRE

GEORGE ORWELL

WALT DISNEY

DOUGLAS ADAMS

JOHN F. KENNEDY

DOROTHY PARKER

ALBERT EINSTEIN

FRANK ZAPPA

NELSON MANDELA

OSCAR WILDE

MARGARET THATCHER

PABLO PICASSO
AESOP
LEO TOLSTOY
ORSON WELLES
ISAAC ASIMOV
MARK TWAIN
BUDDHA
GROUCHO MARX
VODEHOUSE
BILL CLINTON
VIRGINIA WOOLF
JANE AUSTEN
SAMUEL PEPYS
W.C. FIELDS
MARILYN MONROE
SHAW

VICES
AND VIRTUES

Right and wrong

> Vices are sometimes only virtues carried to excess.
> **Charles Dickens**

To be absolutely honest, what I feel really bad about is that I don't feel worse. That's the ineffectual liberal's problem in a nutshell.

Michael Frayn

Should we all confess our sins to one another we would laugh together at our lack of originality.

Kahlil Gibran

That to be good is to be happy is not something particularly evident in any of our experiences of real life, yet how badly we want it, and need it, to be true.

Fay Weldon

Do not ask me to be good; just ask me to act as though I were.

Jules Renard

Moral force never dwells in solitude; it will always bring neighbours.

Confucius

About morals, I know only that what is moral is what you feel good after and what is immoral is what you feel bad after.

Ernest Hemingway

Vice is its own reward. It is virtue which, if it is to be marked with consumer appeal, must carry Green Shield stamps.

Quentin Crisp

Never let your **sense of morals** prevent you from doing **what's right.**

Isaac Asimov

Virtue is its own reward.

Ovid

Do what you feel in your heart to be right – for you'll be criticised anyway. You'll be damned if you do, and damned if you don't.

Eleanor Roosevelt

To have a right to do a thing is not at all the same as to be right in doing it.

G.K. Chesterton

If a man calls himself a realist, you can be sure he's about to do something he's ashamed of.

Sydney J. Harris

When a stupid man is doing something he's ashamed of, he always declares that it is his duty.

George Bernard Shaw

In matters of style, swim with the current; in matters of principle, stand like a rock.

Thomas Jefferson

There are no right answers to wrong questions.

Ursula K. Le Guin

Human beings are perhaps never more frightening than when they are convinced beyond doubt that they are right.

Laurens van der Post

The only correct actions are those that demand no explanation and no apology.

Red Auerbach

In my day there were things that were done and things that were not done. And there was even a way of doing things that were not done.

Peter Ustinov

When everyone is against you, it means that you are absolutely wrong or absolutely right.

Albert Guinon

Refuse to pander to a morbid interest in your own misdeeds. Pick yourself up, be sorry, shake yourself, and go on again.

Evelyn Underhill

Morality is the herd-instinct in the individual.

Friedrich Nietzsche

The oldest, shortest words – 'yes' and 'no' – are those which require the most thought.

Pythagoras

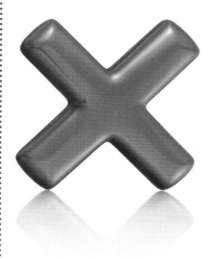

Moral indignation is jealousy with a halo.

H.G. Wells

A thing of beauty

> Remember that the most beautiful things in the world are the most useless; peacocks and lilies, for instance.
>
> **John Ruskin**

Taught from infancy that beauty is a woman's sceptre, the mind shapes itself to the body, and roaming round its gilt cage, only seeks to adorn its prison.

Mary Wollstonecraft

There's nothing more boring than a really beautiful person who has nothing to say.

Gwyneth Paltrow

Beauty is only the promise of happiness.

Stendhal

A thing of beauty is a joy for ever.
Its loveliness increases; it will never
Pass into nothingness.

John Keats

When a woman isn't beautiful, people always say, 'You have lovely eyes, you have lovely hair.'

Anton Chekhov

The psychic scars caused by believing that you are ugly leave a permanent mark on your personality.

Joan Rivers

I'm tired of all this nonsense about beauty being only skin-deep. That's deep enough. What do you want – an adorable pancreas?

Jean Kerr

If you have a great love for beautiful women, then beautiful women will know it.

Roger Vadim

It is easy to be beautiful; it is difficult to appear so.

Hosea Ballou

Character contributes to beauty. It fortifies a woman as her youth fades. A mode of conduct, a standard of courage, discipline, fortitude and integrity can do a great deal to make a woman beautiful.

Jacqueline Bissett

Beauty is all very well at first sight, but who ever looks at it when it has been in the house three days?

George Bernard Shaw

Beauty is eternity gazing at itself in a mirror.

Kahlil Gibran

'Beauty' is a currency system like the gold standard. Like any economy, it is determined by politics, and in the modern age in the West it is the last, best belief system that keeps male dominance intact.

Naomi Wolf

The secret of ugliness consists not in irregularity, but in being uninteresting.

Ralph Waldo Emerson

No matter what a woman looks like, if she's confident, she's sexy.

Paris Hilton

The awful thing is that beauty is mysterious as well as terrible. God and devil are fighting there, and the battlefield is the heart of man.

Fedor Dostoevsky

It is amazing how complete is the delusion that beauty is goodness.

Leo Tolstoy

Love built on beauty, soon as beauty, dies.

John Donne

Too many people say 'beautiful' when they mean 'pretty'. To me, a hippopotamus is beautiful. I much prefer them to swans.

Henry Moore

The trouble with beauty is that it is like being born rich and getting poorer.
Joan Collins

Beauty is in the eye of the beholder and it may be necessary from time to time to give a stupid or misinformed beholder a black eye.
Miss Piggy

Intelligent life

An intellectual is a person who has discovered something more interesting than sex.

Aldous Huxley

The only thing the good Lord has distributed fairly is Intelligence. Everyone is quite sure that they have more of it than anyone else.

Samuel Johnson

The next best thing to being clever is being able to quote someone who is.

Mary Pettibone Poole

The third-rate mind is only happy when it is thinking with the majority. The second-rate mind is only happy when it is thinking with the minority, and the first-rate mind is only happy when it is thinking.

A.A. Milne

True intelligence very readily conceives of an intelligence superior to its own; and that is why truly intelligent men are modest.

André Gide

If a little knowledge is dangerous, where is the man who has so much as to be out of danger?

Thomas H. Huxley

You can persuade a man to believe almost anything provided he is clever enough, but it is much more difficult to persuade someone less clever.

Tom Stoppard

Minds are like **parachutes;** they work best when **open.**

Thomas Dewar

Cleverness is serviceable for everything, sufficient for nothing.

Henri Frédéric Amiel

It's easy to forget what intelligence consists of: luck and speculation. Here and there a windfall, here and there a scoop.

John Le Carré

Intelligence is a luxury, sometimes useless, sometimes fatal. It is a torch or a firebrand, according to the use one makes of it.

Fernan Caballero

An intellectual is a man who takes more words than necessary to tell more than he knows.

Dwight D. Eisenhower

The difference between stupid and intelligent people – and this is true whether or not they are well-educated – is that intelligent people can handle subtlety.

Neal Stephenson

My mother said I must always be intolerant of ignorance but understanding of illiteracy. That some people, unable to go to school, were more educated and more intelligent than college professors.

Maya Angelou

Intelligence is really a kind of taste: taste in ideas.

Susan Sontag

There are three kinds of intelligence: one kind understands things for itself, the other appreciates what others can understand, the third understands neither for itself nor through others. This first kind is excellent, the second good and the third kind useless.

Niccolò Machiavelli

A minute's thought would have shown him that it could not be true. But a minute is a long time and thought is difficult.

A.E. Housman

If we listened to our intellect, we'd never have a love affair. We'd never have a friendship. We'd never go into business, because we'd be cynical. Well, that's nonsense. You've got to jump off cliffs all the time and build your wings on the way down.

Ray Bradbury

The test of a first-rate intelligence is the ability to hold two opposed ideas in the mind at the same time, and still retain the ability to function.

F. Scott Fitzgerald

Sir, I have found you an argument; but I am not obliged to find you an understanding.

Samuel Johnson

I have never met a man so ignorant that I couldn't learn something from him.
Galileo

Courage and bravery

When it comes to the pinch, human beings are heroic.
George Orwell

There's no such thing as bravery, only degrees of fear.
John Wainwright

There are all kinds of courage. It takes a great deal of bravery to stand up to our enemies, but just as much to stand up to our friends.
J.K. Rowling

Courage is doing what you're afraid to do. There can be no courage unless you're scared.
Eddie Rickenbacker

Courage – fear that has said its prayers.
Dorothy Bernard

Courage is not merely one of the virtues but the form of every virtue at the testing point, which means at the point of highest reality.
C.S. Lewis

The only courage that matters is the kind that gets you from one moment to the next.
Mignon McLaughlin

People with courage and character always seem sinister to the rest.
Hermann Hesse

Courage is what it takes to stand up and speak; courage is also what it takes to sit down and listen.
Winston Churchill

Fortune favours the brave.
Virgil

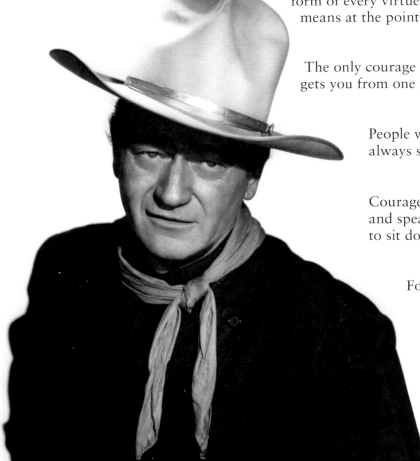

Courage is being scared to death – but saddling up anyway.
John Wayne

He who loses wealth loses much; he who loses a friend loses more; but he that loses his courage loses all.

Miguel de Cervantes

Success is that old ABC – ability, breaks and courage.

Charles Luckman

Boldness be my friend!
Arm me, audacity.

William Shakespeare

Courage is fire, and bullying is smoke.

Benjamin Disraeli

Anyone who has gumption knows what it is, and anyone who hasn't can never know what it is. So there is no need of defining it.

L.M. Montgomery

What counts is not necessarily the size of the dog in the fight – it's the size of the fight in the dog.

Dwight D. Eisenhower

Courage
is grace under
pressure.
Ernest Hemingway

Courage is the art of being the only one who knows you're scared to death.

Harold Wilson

A great deal of talent is lost to the world for want of a little courage. Every day sends to their graves obscure men whose timidity prevented them from making a first effort.

Sydney Smith

The only thing we have to fear is fear itself.

Franklin D. Roosevelt

The important thing is this: to be able at any moment to sacrifice what we are for what we could become.

Charles Du Bos

Take a chance! All life is a chance. The man who goes furthest is generally the one who is willing to do and dare.

Dale Carnegie

Oscar Wilde

THE VERY SOUL OF WIT

Looking back on his life from his prison cell in Reading Gaol, serving two years hard labour for gross indecency, Oscar Fingal O'Flahertie Wills Wilde wrote that he was once 'a lord of language' who 'summed up all systems in a phrase and all existence in an epigram'. Contained within his literary genius was the miniaturist's gift for compression: he could be witty, profound, thoughtful or irreverent in a few exquisitely chosen words.

Wilde was fond of presenting apparent contradictions as if they were eternal truths: 'The only difference between a caprice and lifelong passion is that the caprice lasts a little longer.' He also enjoyed fashioning doublets in which the second part of the thought is a reflection or a reversal of the first: 'I always like to know everything about my new friends, and nothing about my old ones.' He made many sharply brittle remarks about pleasure, art and the joys of art – among which is the untypically unequivocal observation that 'all art is quite useless'.

But Wilde's witticisms were never mere word-games. It is truer to say that they were philosophical experiments. As a character in one of his plays remarks: 'The way of paradoxes is the way of Truth. To test Reality we must see it on the tight-rope. When the Verities become acrobats, then we can judge them.'

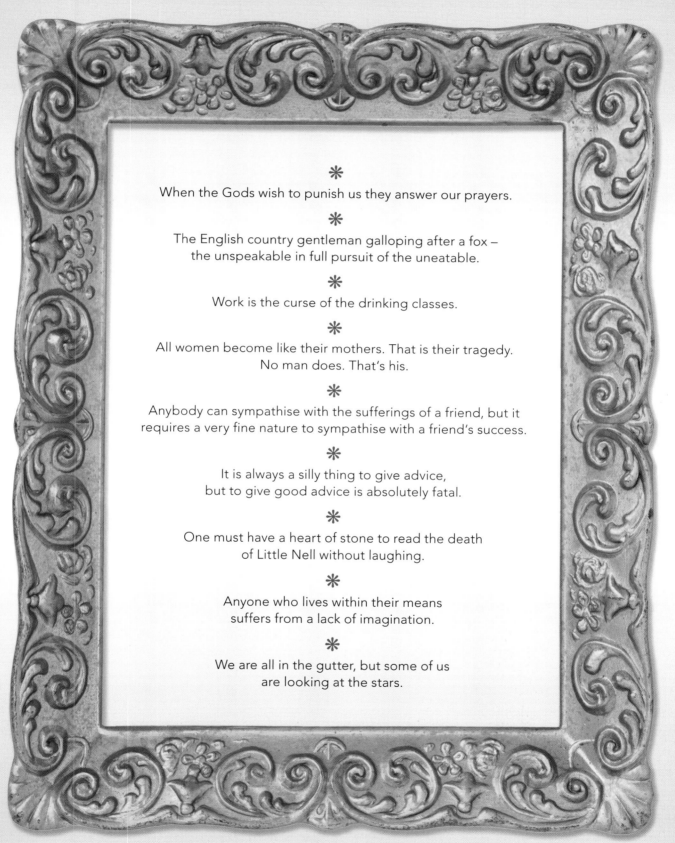

✳

When the Gods wish to punish us they answer our prayers.

✳

The English country gentleman galloping after a fox –
the unspeakable in full pursuit of the uneatable.

✳

Work is the curse of the drinking classes.

✳

All women become like their mothers. That is their tragedy.
No man does. That's his.

✳

Anybody can sympathise with the sufferings of a friend, but it
requires a very fine nature to sympathise with a friend's success.

✳

It is always a silly thing to give advice,
but to give good advice is absolutely fatal.

✳

One must have a heart of stone to read the death
of Little Nell without laughing.

✳

Anyone who lives within their means
suffers from a lack of imagination.

✳

We are all in the gutter, but some of us
are looking at the stars.

Strength and weakness

I learned that it is the weak who are cruel, and that gentleness is to be expected only from the strong.

Leo Rosten

Human nature is such that the spectacle of another's weakness awakens even in the best of us a feeling of power which contains along with the sincerest pity, an almost imperceptible mingling of pleasure.

André Maurois

At 15 life had taught me undeniably that surrender, in its place, was as honourable as resistance, especially if one had no choice.

Maya Angelou

On close inspection, the beast within us looks suspiciously like a sheep.

Sarah J. McCarthy

Build up your weaknesses until they become your strong points.

Knute Rockne

There are few of us who have not a strong propensity to diminish our present strength by entertaining fears of future weakness.

Charles B. Fairbanks

Rudeness is the weak man's imitation of strength.

Eric Hoffer

I am extraordinarily patient provided I get my own way in the end.

Margaret Thatcher

Tears shed for self are tears of weakness, but tears shed for others are a sign of strength.

Billy Graham

You gain strength, courage and confidence by every experience in which you really stop to look fear in the face. You are able to say to yourself, 'I have lived through this horror. I can take the next thing that comes along.' You must do the thing you think you cannot do.

Eleanor Roosevelt

If you can't stand the heat, get out of the kitchen.

Harry S Truman

Blessed are the meek: for they shall inherit the earth.
The Bible
(Gospel of Matthew)

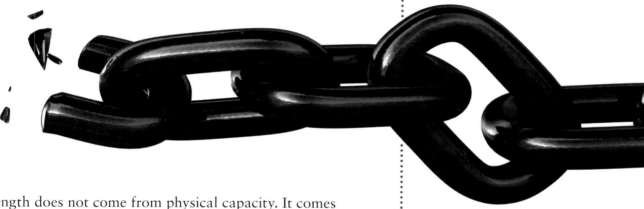

Strength does not come from physical capacity. It comes from an indomitable will.

Mahatma Gandhi

You cannot have force in two places at the same time; and you must know a man's weakness before you truly know his strength.

Havelock Ellis

The weak are strong because they are reckless. The strong are weak because they have scruples.

Otto von Bismarck

The strong man is strongest when alone.

Friedrich Schiller

We like to know the weakness of eminent men; it consoles us for our inferiority.

Madame de Lambert

I know I have but the body of a weak and feeble woman; but I have the heart of a king, and of a king of England, too.

Queen Elizabeth I

Kindness and generosity

> You cannot shake hands with a clenched fist.
> **Indira Gandhi**

We who lived in concentration camps can remember the men who walked through the huts comforting others, giving away their last piece of bread. They may have been few in number, but they offer sufficient proof that everything can be taken from a man but one thing: the last of human freedoms – to choose one's attitude in any given set of circumstances – to choose one's own way.

Viktor E. Frankl

From what we get, we can make a living; what we give, however, makes a life.

Arthur Ashe

If a man be gracious and courteous to strangers, it shows he is a citizen of the world, and that his heart is no island cut off from other lands, but a continent that joins to them.

Francis Bacon

You must give some time to your fellow men. Even if it's a little thing, do something for others – something for which you get no pay but the privilege of doing it.

Albert Schweitzer

Givers have to set limits because takers rarely do.

Irma Kurtz

How wonderful it is that nobody need wait a single moment before starting to improve the world.

Anne Frank

Beginning today, treat everyone you meet as if they were going to be dead by midnight. Extend them all the care, kindness and understanding you can muster. Your life will never be the same again.

Og Mandino

No good deed goes unpunished.

Clare Boothe Luce

'Tis more blessed to give than receive; for example, wedding presents.

H.L. Mencken

After the verb 'to love', 'to help' is the most beautiful
verb in the world.

Bertha von Suttner

The smallest deed is better than the greatest intention.

John Burroughs

No one would remember the Good Samaritan if he'd only
had good intentions – he had money as well.

Margaret Thatcher

If you find it in your heart to
care for somebody else, you
will have succeeded.

Maya Angelou

Never look down on anybody
unless you're helping him up.

Jesse Jackson

Too often we underestimate the power of a touch, a smile,
a kind word, a listening ear, an honest compliment, or the
smallest act of caring, all of which have the potential to
turn a life around.

Leo Buscaglia

In charity there is no excess.

Francis Bacon

I don't think there's any richer reward in life than helping
someone. You can't measure it in money or fame or
anything else. But if we're not put here for anything else
but to help each other get through life, I think that's a
very honourable existence.

Tom Brokaw

What we have done for ourselves alone dies with us;
what we have done for others and the world remains
and is immortal.

Albert Pike

We cannot hold a torch to light another's path without
brightening our own.

Ben Sweetland

The service we render to others is really the rent we pay
for our room on this earth.

Wilfred Grenfell

A day wasted
on others is not
wasted on one's self.

Charles Dickens

Anger and hatred

No one is born hating another person because of the colour of his skin, or his background, or his religion. People must learn to hate, and if they can learn to hate, they can be taught to love, for love comes more naturally to the human heart than its opposite.

Nelson Mandela

Let not the sun go down upon your wrath.

The Bible (Ephesians)

Hating gets going, it goes round, it gets older and tighter and older and tighter, until it holds a person inside it like a fist holds a stick.

Ursula K. Le Guin

Anger makes dull men witty, but it keeps them poor.

Francis Bacon

I know of no more disagreeable sensation than to be left feeling generally angry without anybody in particular to be angry at.

Frank Moore Colby

A soft answer turneth away wrath.

The Bible (Proverbs)

Hate has what lust entirely lacks – persistence and continuity: the persistence and continuity of purposive spirit.

Aldous Huxley

We boil at different degrees.

Clint Eastwood

My loathings are simple: stupidity, oppression, crime, cruelty, soft music.

Vladimir Nabokov

Never leave a message in haste or anger.

Jeff Davidson

I don't have pet peeves, I have whole kennels of irritation.

Whoopi Goldberg

I know that there are people who do not love their fellow man, and I hate people like that!

Tom Lehrer

As long as you hate, there will be people to hate.

George Harrison

I hate mankind, for I think myself one of the best of them, and I know how bad I am.

James Boswell

Fear of something is at the root of hate for others, and hate within will eventually destroy the hater.

George Washington Carver

Anger and jealousy can no more bear to lose sight of their objects than love.

George Eliot

I do not want people to be agreeable, as it saves me the trouble of liking them.

Jane Austen

Hatred is self-punishment. Hatred is the coward's revenge for being intimidated.

Hosea Ballou

The world needs anger. The world often continues to allow evil because it isn't angry enough.

Bede Jarrett

If you hate a person, you hate something in him that is part of yourself. What isn't part of ourselves doesn't disturb us.

Hermann Hesse

It's my rule never to lose me temper till it would be detrimental to keep it.

Sean O'Casey

Hate must make a man productive. Otherwise one might as well love.

Karl Kraus

Temper is a weapon that we hold by the blade.

J.M. Barrie

Fear and worry

Fear is that little darkroom where negatives are developed.

Michael Pritchard

It takes a real storm in the average person's life to make him realise how much worrying he has done over the squalls.

Bruce Barton

Feel the fear and do it anyway.

Susan Jeffers

Take therefore no thought for the morrow: for the morrow shall take thought for the things of itself. Sufficient unto the day is the evil thereof.

The Bible (Gospel of Matthew)

People should worry about each other. Because worry is just love in its worst form. But it's still love.

Simon Gray

To fear love is to fear life, and those who fear life are already three parts dead.

Bertrand Russell

If I knew what I was so anxious about, I wouldn't be so anxious.

Mignon McLaughlin

Anxiety is love's greatest killer. It makes others feel as you might when a drowning man holds on to you. You want to save him, but you know he will strangle you with his panic.

Anaïs Nin

People are never more insecure than when they become obsessed with their fears at the expense of their dreams.

Norman Cousins

For the most part, fear is nothing but an illusion. When you share it with someone else, it tends to disappear.

Marilyn C. Barrick

Worry never robs tomorrow of its sorrow, it only saps today of its joy.

Leo Buscaglia

Do the thing you fear to do and keep on doing it ...
that is the quickest and surest way ever yet discovered
to conquer fear.

Dale Carnegie

If you see ten troubles coming down the road, you can be
sure that nine will run into the ditch before they reach you.

Calvin Coolidge

The mass of men lead lives of quiet desperation. What is
called resignation is confirmed desperation.

Henry David Thoreau

Nowadays men lead lives of noisy desperation.

James Thurber

The reason why worry kills more people than work is that
more people worry than work.

Robert Frost

Fear is a disease that eats
away at logic and makes
man inhuman.

Marian Anderson

Uneasy lies the head that wears a crown.

William Shakespeare

There are only three sins – causing pain, causing fear
and causing anguish. The rest is window dressing.

Roger Caras

Worry is impatience.

Austin O'Malley

No passion so effectually robs the mind of all its powers of
acting and reasoning as fear.

Edmund Burke

Nothing puzzles me more than time and space; and yet
nothing troubles me less, as I never think about them.

Charles Lamb

Worry is interest paid on trouble before it falls due.

William Ralph Inge

A ruffled mind makes
a restless pillow.
Charlotte Brontë

As a cure for **worrying**, work is
better than whiskey.

Ralph Waldo Emerson

Pride and humility

If I only had
a little humility,
I'd be perfect.

Ted Turner

Early in life I had to choose between honest arrogance and hypocritical humility. I chose honest arrogance and have seen no occasion to change it.

Frank Lloyd Wright

Humility does not consist in an ignorance of truth. When a man is above the average height of man, he cannot help knowing it.

Cardinal Henry Manning

I don't do humble.

Robert Kilroy-Silk

When will you be humble enough not to be afraid of anyone thinking this or that of you, even if it be something good?

Maurice Lesage d'Hautecoeur d'Hulst

Only the man with true pride in his capacities as a human being can have a significant humility; only the truly humble in apprehending the immensity of the universe and the world beyond himself can have a significant pride – a sense of his own identity.

Helen Merrell Lynd

Pride goeth before destruction, and an haughty spirit before a fall.

The Bible (Proverbs)

If I'm ever feeling a bit uppity, whenever I get on my high horse, I go and take another look at my dear Mam's mangle that has pride of place in the dining-room.

Brian Clough

I have often wished I had time to cultivate modesty ... but I am too busy thinking about myself.

Edith Sitwell

As for conceit, what man will do any good who is not conceited? Nobody holds a good opinion of a man who has a low opinion of himself.

Anthony Trollope

It is far more impressive when others discover your good qualities without your help.

Judith Martin

Egotist: A person more interested in himself than in me.

Ambrose Bierce

Shyness has a strange element of narcissism, a belief that how we look, how we perform, is truly important to other people.

Andre Dubus

He that is proud eats up himself; pride in his glass, his trumpet, his chronicle; and whatever praises itself but in the deed, devours the deed in the praise.

William Shakespeare

The nice thing about egotists is that they don't talk about other people.

Lucille S. Harper

Vanity and pride are different things, though the words are often used synonymously. A person may be proud without being vain. Pride relates more to our opinion of ourselves, vanity to what we would have others think of us.

Jane Austen

Noise proves nothing. Often a hen who has merely laid an egg cackles as if she had laid an asteroid.

Mark Twain

Talk to a man about himself, and he will listen for hours.

Benjamin Disraeli

If you think you are not conceited, it means you're very conceited indeed.

C.S. Lewis

Nothing is so silly as the expression of a man being complimented.

André Gide

Shyness is egotism out of its depth.
Penelope Keith

In 1969, I published a small book on Humility. It was a pioneering work which has not, to my knowledge, been superseded.

Lord Longford

The sharpest epitaphs

Why leave your last words to chance, when you can prepare for eternity with some well-turned phrases to be inscribed at your final resting place? Many great names have used the opportunity to inspire and amuse us from beyond the grave.

The only proof he needed for the existence of God was music.
Kurt Vonnegut

Curiosity did not kill this cat.
Studs Terkel

I had a lover's quarrel with the world.
Robert Frost

Where fierce indignation can no longer tear his heart.
Jonathan Swift

A tomb now suffices him for whom the world was not enough.
Alexander the Great

Here lies one whose name was writ in water.
John Keats

Do not walk on the grass.
Peter Ustinov

She did it the hard way.
Bette Davis

This is the last of Earth! I am content!
John Quincy Adams

Free at last. Free at last. Thank God Almighty, I'm free at last.
Martin Luther King, Jnr

Now he belongs to the ages.
Abraham Lincoln

The body of B. Franklin, printer,
Like the cover of an old book
Its contents torn out
And stripped of its lettering and guilding
Lies here food for worms
For it will, as he believed, appear once more
In a new and more elegant edition
Corrected and improved by the Author.

Benjamin Franklin

174517
Primo Levi (citing the number that was
tattooed on his arm at Auschwitz)

That's all, folks.
Mel Blanc (voice of Bugs Bunny,
Daffy Duck and Porky Pig)

For tho' from out our bourne of Time and Place
The flood may bear me far,
I hope to see my Pilot face to face
When I have crossed the bar.

Alfred, Lord Tennyson

Workers of all lands unite.
Karl Marx

May my husband rest in peace till I get there.
Dame Edna Everage

I told you I was ill.
Spike Milligan

Good friend, for Jesu's sake forbear,
To dig the dust enclosed here.
Blest be the man that spares these stones,
But cursed be he that moves my bones.

William Shakespeare

Forgiveness and compassion

> The secret of forgiving everything is to understand nothing.
> **George Bernard Shaw**

I believe any person who asks for forgiveness has to be prepared to give it.

Bill Clinton

The stupid neither forgive nor forget; the naïve forgive and forget; the wise forgive but do not forget.

Thomas Szasz

Know all, and you will pardon all.

Thomas à Kempis

Whenever anyone has offended me, I try to raise my soul so high that the offence cannot reach it.

René Descartes

Distrust all in whom the impulse to punish is powerful!

Friedrich Nietzsche

They may forget what you said, but they will never forget how you made them feel.

Carl W. Buechner

Forgiveness does not change the past, but it does enlarge the future.

Paul Boese

If you overpower your enemy, then pardon him by way of thankfulness to Allah, for being able to subdue him.

Ali ibn Abi Talib

If you want others to be happy, practise compassion. If you want to be happy, practise compassion.

Dalai Lama

The quality of mercy is not strain'd; it droppeth as the gentle rain from heaven upon the place beneath. It is twice blest: it blesseth him that gives and him that takes.

William Shakespeare

Women don't forgive failure.

Anton Chekhov

He who demands mercy and shows none burns the bridges over which he himself must later pass.

Thomas Adams

Forget injuries; never forget kindnesses.

Confucius

One thing you will **probably remember** well is any time you forgive and forget.

Franklin P. Jones

Life appears to me too short to be spent in nursing animosity or registering wrongs.

Charlotte Brontë

Pity is for the living, envy is for the dead.

Mark Twain

You cannot go around and keep score. If you keep score on the good things and the bad things, you'll find out that you're a very miserable person. God gave man the ability to forget, which is one of the greatest attributes you have. Because if you remember everything that's happened to you, you generally remember that which is the most unfortunate.

Hubert H. Humphrey

Forgiveness is almost a selfish act because of its immense benefits to the one who forgives.

Lawana Blackwell

Holding on to anger, resentment and hurt only gives you tense muscles, a headache and a sore jaw from clenching your teeth. Forgiveness gives you back the laughter and the lightness in your life.

Joan Lunden

Forgiveness is a virtue of the brave.

Indira Gandhi

We never forgive those who make us blush.

Jean-François de La Harpe

Hope and despair

In a real dark night of the soul, it is always 3 o'clock in the morning, day after day.

F. Scott Fitzgerald

Hope is definitely not the same thing as optimism. It is not the conviction that something will turn out well, but the certainty that something makes sense, regardless of how it turns out.

Václav Havel

Tomorrow is another day.

Margaret Mitchell

I give the fight up: let there be an end,
A privacy, an obscure nook for me.
I want to be forgotten even by God.

Robert Browning

In despair there are the most intense enjoyments, especially when one is very acutely conscious of the hopelessness of one's position.

Fedor Dostoevsky

The human mind can bear plenty of reality, but not too much unintermittent gloom.

Margaret Drabble

Hope is the thing with feathers that perches in the soul.

Emily Dickinson

I find hope in the darkest of days, and focus in the brightest. I do not judge the universe.

Dalai Lama

Despair is the price one pays for setting oneself an impossible aim.

Graham Greene

A hope, if it is not big enough, can poison much more thoroughly than most despairs, for hope is more essentially an irritant than a soporific.

William Bolitho

Everywhere I see bliss, from which I alone am irrevocably excluded.

Mary Shelley

Hope begins in the dark, the stubborn hope that if you just show up and try to do the right thing, the dawn will come.

Anne Lamott

In all disagreeable circumstances remember the three things which I always say to myself: I am an Englishwoman. I was born in wedlock. I am on dry land.

Blanche Warre Cornish

Hope is only the love of life.

Henri Frédéric Amiel

No cause is hopeless. Things have a way of bringing about their antithesis, of surprising us radically.

Joyce Carol Oates

I once counselled a man in despair to do what I myself did in similar circumstances: to live for short terms. Come, I said to myself at that time, at any rate you can bear it for a quarter of an hour!

Theodor Haecker

I hate despair. I find it intolerable. The stink of it gets up my nose. It's a blemish. Despair, old fruit, is a cancer. It should be castrated. Indeed I've often found that that works. Chop the balls off and despair goes out the window.

Harold Pinter

A dead end can never be a one-way street; you can always turn around and take another road.

Bo Bennett

If you're going through hell, keep going.

Walt Disney

Our doubts are traitors, and make us lose the good we oft might win, by fearing to attempt.

William Shakespeare

Human life begins on the far side of despair.

Jean-Paul Sartre

Hope is the feeling you have that the feeling you have isn't permanent.

Jean Kerr

Honesty and deceit

It is discouraging how many people are shocked by honesty and how few by deceit.

Noël Coward

I lie altruistically – for our mutual good. The lie is the basic building block of good manners. That may seem mildly shocking to a moralist – but then what isn't?

Quentin Crisp

Oh what a tangled web we weave,
When first we practice to deceive!

Walter Scott

Suspect all extraordinary and groundless civilities.

Thomas Fuller

A man who trusts nobody is apt to be the kind of man nobody trusts.

Harold Macmillan

I do not mind lying, but I hate inaccuracy.

Samuel Butler

Exaggeration is a blood relation to falsehood and nearly as blameable.

Hosea Ballou

It is hard to believe that a man is telling the truth when you know that you would lie if you were in his place.

H.L. Mencken

An honest man is the noblest work of God.

Alexander Pope

You can fool some of the people all of the time, and all of the people some of the time, but you cannot fool all of the people all of the time.

Abraham Lincoln

There are a terrible lot of lies going around the world, and the worst of it is half of them are true.

Winston Churchill

Never trust a person who says 'frankly', 'candidly' or 'to be honest.' He probably is none of those things.

Roger Simon

Fair speech may hide a foul heart.

J.R.R. Tolkien

A man always has two reasons for doing anything: a good reason and the real reason.

J.P. Morgan

Several excuses are always less convincing than one.

Aldous Huxley

It is always the best policy to speak the truth, unless, of course, you are an exceptionally good liar.

Jerome K. Jerome

When you want to fool the world, tell the truth.
Otto von Bismarck

Lying to ourselves is more deeply ingrained than lying to others.
Fedor Dostoevsky

Sin has **many tools,** but a lie is **the handle** which fits them all.

Edmund Burke

The best measure of a man's honesty isn't his income tax return. It's the zero adjust on his bathroom scale.

Arthur C. Clarke

I believe in trusting. Trust begets trust. Suspicion is fetid and only stinks. He who trusts has never yet lost in the world.

Mahatma Gandhi

We only admit our little faults to persuade others we have no great ones.

Duc de la Rochefoucauld

Doubtless the pleasure is as great
Of being cheated, as to cheat.
As lookers-on feel most delight,
That least perceive a juggler's sleight.

Samuel Butler

Stupidity and ignorance

There's nothing more dangerous than a resourceful idiot.

Scott Adams

Only two things are infinite, the universe and human stupidity, and I'm not sure about the former.

Albert Einstein

I am patient with stupidity but not with those who are proud of it.

Edith Sitwell

With stupidity the gods themselves struggle in vain.

Friedrich Schiller

In view of the fact that God limited the intelligence of man, it seems unfair that He did not also limit his stupidity.

Konrad Adenauer

Aristotle was famous for knowing everything. He taught that the brain exists merely to cool the blood and is not involved in the process of thinking. This is true only of certain persons.

Will Cuppy

Ignorance is like a delicate exotic fruit; touch it and the bloom is gone.

Oscar Wilde

He may look like an idiot and talk like an idiot but don't let that fool you. He really is an idiot.

Groucho Marx

A foolish consistency is the hobgoblin of little minds, adored by little statesmen and philosophers and divines.

Ralph Waldo Emerson

Stupidity is an elemental force for which no earthquake is a match.

Karl Kraus

Little-minded people's thoughts move in such small circles that 5 minutes' conversation gives you an arc long enough to determine their whole curve.

Oliver Wendell Holmes

Behind every argument is someone's ignorance.

Louis D. Brandeis

One man alone can be pretty dumb sometimes, but for real bona fide stupidity, there ain't nothin' can beat teamwork.

Edward Abbey

Against logic there is no armour like ignorance.

Laurence J. Peter

Genuine ignorance is profitable because it is likely to be accompanied by humility, curiosity and open mindedness; whereas ability to repeat catch-phrases, cant terms, familiar propositions, gives the conceit of learning and coats the mind with varnish waterproof to new ideas.

John Dewey

Ignorance gives one a large range of probabilities.

George Eliot

Half the world is composed of idiots, the other half of people clever enough to take indecent advantage of them.

Walter Kerr

The best way to convince a fool that he is wrong is to let him have his own way.

Josh Billings

Ignorance is not innocence but sin.

Robert Browning

A great many people think they are thinking when they are merely rearranging their prejudices.

William James

There are two ways to slide easily through life; to believe everything or to doubt everything. Both ways save us from thinking.

Alfred Korzybski

If one does not know to which port one is sailing, no wind is favourable.

Seneca

There is more stupidity around than hydrogen and it has a longer shelf life.

Frank Zappa

Talent and creativity

Originality is unexplored territory. You get there by carrying a canoe – you can't take a taxi.
Alan Alda

Keep on going and the chances are you will stumble on something, perhaps when you are least expecting it. I have never heard of anyone stumbling on something sitting down.
Charles F. Kettering

One sits down first; one thinks afterwards.
Jean Cocteau

Creative powers may go with an intellect not, in other ways, very bright ... In the human world, nightingales can be geese.
F.L. Lucas

The very essence of the creative is its novelty, and hence we have no standard by which to judge it.
Carl R. Rogers

Where talent is a dwarf, self-esteem is a giant.
Jean Antoine Petit-Senn

No man can discover his own talents.
Brendan Francis

If a man has a talent and cannot use it, he has failed. If he has a talent and uses only half of it, he has partly failed. If he has a talent and learns somehow to use the whole of it, he has gloriously succeeded, and won a satisfaction and a triumph that few men ever know.
Thomas Wolfe

Creativity is the ability to see relationships where none exist.
Thomas Disch

Our current obsession with creativity is the result of our continued striving for immortality in an era when most people no longer believe in an afterlife.
Arianna Huffington

Once in seven years I burn all my sermons; for it is a shame if I cannot write better sermons now than I did seven years ago.

John Wesley

Talent is nothing but a prolonged period of attention and a shortened period of mental assimiliation.

Konstantin Stanislavsky

When inspiration does not come to me, I go halfway to meet it.

Sigmund Freud

The creative adult is the child who has survived.

Ursula K. Le Guin

A talent somewhat above mediocrity, shrewd and not too sensitive, is more likely to rise in the world than genius, which is apt to be perturbable and to wear itself out before fruition.

Charles Horton Cooley

Creativity can solve almost any problem. The creative act, the defeat of habit by originality, overcomes everything.

George Lois

A hunch is creativity trying to tell you something.
Frank Capra

The secret to creativity is knowing how to hide your sources.
Albert Einstein

There are two kinds of people, those who **finish what they start** and so on.

Robert Byrne

Creativity requires the courage to let go of certainties.

Erich Fromm

Curiosity about life in all of its aspects, I think, is still the secret of great creative people.

Leo Burnett

The opposite of creativity is cynicism.

Esa Saarinen

If you have great talents, industry will improve them: if you have but moderate abilities, industry will supply their deficiency.

Joshua Reynolds

Whom the gods wish to destroy they first call promising.
Cyril Connolly

Mahatma Gandhi

THE PEACEFUL REVOLUTIONARY

Mohandas Karamchand Gandhi combined the roles of spiritual leader and politician, and he used his spiritual principles to achieve his political ends. He was for decades the figurehead of India's struggle for independence from Britain. The weapons he chose to use in this fight were passive resistance, non-cooperation, civil disobedience and – above all – non-violence. 'There are many causes that I am prepared to die for,' he said, 'but no causes that I am prepared to kill for.'

The British establishment despised Gandhi. Winston Churchill dismissed him as 'a seditious middle temple lawyer, now posing as a fakir of a type well known in the east'. The authorities in India repeatedly threw him in prison, but could not dent his moral authority. Gandhi's own people, India's poor and dispossessed millions, revered him as 'Bapu' – 'Father'; and the poet Rabindranath Tagore endowed him with the epithet 'Mahatma' or 'Great Soul'.

After the Second World War it fell to Gandhi to lead India to independence. But he was appalled by the unstoppable violence that the process unleashed between India's faith communities, particularly Hindus, Muslims and Sikhs. He himself became a victim of religious fanaticism: a Hindu extremist shot him dead in 1948. 'What I have done will endure,' said Gandhi. 'Not what I have said or written.'

I hate privilege and monopoly. Whatever cannot be
shared with the masses is taboo to me.

Whenever I see an erring man, I say to myself I have also erred;
when I see a lustful man, I say to myself so was I once;
and in this way, I feel kinship with everyone in the world and
feel that I cannot be happy without the humblest of us being happy.

I cannot intentionally hurt anything that lives,
much less fellow human beings, even though they may
do the greatest wrong to me and mine.

I shall have to answer my God and my Maker if I give anyone
less than his due, but I am sure that He will bless me if
He knows that I gave someone more than his due.

You must not lose faith in humanity. Humanity is an ocean; if a few drops
of the ocean are dirty, the ocean does not become dirty.

Mere brave speech without action is letting off useless steam.

Whatever you do will be insignificant,
but it is very important that you do it.

There are moments in your life when you must act, even though you cannot
carry your best friends with you. The 'still small voice' within you must
always be the final arbiter when there is a conflict of duty.

You must be the change you want to see in the world.

Ethical living

The Ten Commandments should be treated like an examination. Only six need to be attempted.

Bertrand Russell

If we aren't willing to pay a price for our values, then we should ask ourselves whether we truly believe in them at all.

Barack Obama

To try to be better is to be better.

Charlotte Cushman

The true test of character is not how much we know how to do, but how we behave when we don't know what to do.

John Holt

Our character is what we do when we think no one is looking.

H. Jackson Brown

Good humour is one of the best articles of dress one can wear in society.

William Makepeace Thackeray

We are here on earth to do good to others. What the others are here for, I don't know.

W.H. Auden

The problem with people who have no vices is that generally you can be pretty sure they're going to have some pretty annoying virtues.

Elizabeth Taylor

There are two cardinal sins from which all the others spring: impatience and laziness.

Franz Kafka

The ultimate test of man's conscience may be his willingness to sacrifice something today for future generations whose words of thanks will not be heard.

Gaylord Nelson

Be not too hasty to trust or admire the teachers of morality: they discourse like angels but they live like men.

Samuel Johnson

Underneath this flabby exterior is an enormous lack of character.

Oscar Levant

The good should be grateful to the bad – for providing the world with a basis for comparison.

Sven Halla

Lead me not into temptation; I can find the way myself.

Rita Mae Brown

Those are my **principles.**
If you don't like them, I have others.

Groucho Marx

We are all selfish and I no more trust myself than others with a good motive.

Lord Byron

I have but one idea, which was an idea that I inherited, and it was the idea of service. All my life I believed from my heart the words of Browning: 'All service ranks the same with God'. It makes very little difference whether a man is driving a tramcar or sweeping streets or being prime minister, if he only brings to that service everything that is in him and performs it for the sake of mankind.

Stanley Baldwin

I have gained this by philosophy: that I do without being commanded what others do only from fear of the law.

Aristotle

The only reward of virtue is virtue; the only way to have a friend is to be one.

Ralph Waldo Emerson

Being good is just a matter of temperament in the end.

Iris Murdoch

It is good to be without vices, but it is not good to be without temptations.

Walter Bagehot

The nation's morals are like its teeth: the more decayed they are the more it hurts to touch them.

George Bernard Shaw

The wages of sin are death, but by the time taxes are taken out, it's just sort of a tired feeling.

Paula Poundstone

Action and inaction

The important work of moving the world forward does not wait to be done by perfect men.

George Eliot

There are risks and costs to a programme of action. But they are far less than the long-range risks and costs of comfortable inaction.

John F. Kennedy

The most dangerous strategy is to jump a chasm in two leaps.

Benjamin Disraeli

Be wary of the man who urges an action in which he himself incurs no risk.

Joaquin Setanti

A thought which does not result in an action is nothing much, and an action which does not proceed from a thought is nothing at all.

Georges Bernanos

Every action of our lives touches on some chord that will vibrate in eternity.

Sean O'Casey

The way to get started is to quit talking and begin doing.

Walt Disney

Be always sure you are right – then go ahead.

Davy Crockett

Each time someone stands up for an ideal, or acts to improve the lot of others, or strikes out against injustice, he sends forth a tiny ripple of hope.

Robert F. Kennedy

The darkest places in hell are reserved for those who maintain their neutrality in times of moral crisis.

Dante Alighieri

Neutrality helps the oppressor, never the victim. Silence encourages the tormentor, never the tormented.

Elie Wiesel

I have learned, as a rule of thumb, never to ask whether you can do something. Say, instead, that you are doing it. Then fasten your seat belt. The most remarkable things follow.

Julia Cameron

To try and find out the reason for everything is very dangerous and leads to nothing but disappointment.

Queen Victoria

A little knowledge that acts is worth infinitely more than much knowledge that is idle.

Kahlil Gibran

A thousand words will not leave so deep an impression as one deed.

Henrik Ibsen

When you strike at a king, you must kill him.

Ralph Waldo Emerson

No one could make a greater mistake than he who did nothing because he could do only a little.

Edmund Burke

The greatest enemy of progress is not stagnation, but false progress.

Sydney J. Harris

The character of every act depends upon the circumstances in which it is done.

Oliver Wendell Holmes

Action is eloquence.

William Shakespeare

It is easy to sit up and take notice. What is difficult is getting up and taking action.

Honoré de Balzac

First they came for the Communists but I was not a Communist so I did not speak out. Then they came for the Socialists and the Trade Unionists but I was not one of them, so I did not speak out. Then they came for the Jews but I was not Jewish so I did not speak out. And when they came for me, there was no one left to speak out for me.

Martin Niemöller

Never mistake motion for action.
Ernest Hemingway

Ambition and motivation

There is no point at which you can say, 'Well, I'm successful now, I might as well take a nap.'

Carrie Fisher

Give me a museum, and I'll fill it.

Pablo Picasso

Ability is what you're capable of doing. Motivation determines what you do. Attitude determines how well you do it.

Lou Holtz

Motivation is when your dreams put on work clothes.

Milton Berle

We need to learn to set our course by the stars, not by the light of every passing ship.

Omar N. Bradley

A somebody was once a nobody who wanted to and did.

John Burroughs

It's never too late to be who you might have been.

George Eliot

Keep away from people who try to belittle your ambitions Small people always do that, but the really great make you feel that you, too, can become great.

Mark Twain

To pretend, I actually do the thing: I have therefore only pretended to pretend.

Jacques Derrida

> Dream as if you'll live forever, live as if you'll die today.
>
> **James Dean**

I am not a has-been.
I am a will-be.

Lauren Bacall

The mind is the limit. As long as the mind can envision the fact that you can do something, you can do it – as long as you really believe 100 per cent.

Arnold Schwarzenegger

I hope that I may always desire more than I can accomplish

Michelangelo

Don't say you don't have enough time. You have exactly the same number of hours per day that were given to Helen Keller, Pasteur, Michelangelo, Mother Teresa, Leonardo da Vinci, Thomas Jefferson and Albert Einstein.

H. Jackson Brown

He is able who thinks he is able.

Buddha

I've always tried to go a step past wherever people expected me to end up.

Beverly Sills

A man with ambition and love for his blessings here on earth is ever so alive. Having been alive, it won't be so hard in the end to lie down and rest.

Pearl Bailey

Well is it known that ambition can creep as well as soar.

Edmund Burke

Achievement is largely the product of steadily raising one's levels of aspiration and expectation.

Jack Nicklaus

Where there is a will, there is a way. If there is a chance in a million that you can do something, anything, to keep what you want from ending, do it. Pry the door open or, if need be, wedge your foot in that door and keep it open.

Pauline Kael

Shoot for the moon. Even if you miss, you'll land among the stars.

Les Brown

No bird soars too high if he soars with his own wings.

William Blake

The most effective way to do it is to do it.
Amelia Earhart

Intelligence without ambition is a bird without wings.

Salvador Dalí

Nose to the grindstone

> If everything seems under control, you're just not going fast enough.
>
> **Mario Andretti**

Humankind is fundamentally idle, and that is one of our real problems.

Princess Anne

Laziness may appear attractive, but work gives satisfaction.

Anne Frank

A great deal of nonsense is talked about the dignity of work. Work is a drug that most people take to avoid the pangs of unmitigated boredom.

W. Somerset Maugham

Diamonds are nothing more than chunks of coal that stuck to their jobs.

Malcolm Forbes

I never could have done what I have done without the habits of punctuality, order and diligence, without the determination to concentrate myself on one subject at a time.

Charles Dickens

Work for something because it is good, not just because it stands a chance to succeed.

Václav Havel

The grass is not, in fact, always greener on the other side of the fence. Fences have nothing to do with it. The grass is greenest where it is watered. When crossing over fences, carry water with you and tend the grass wherever you may be.

Robert Fulghum

I don't think necessity is the mother of invention. Invention, in my opinion, arises directly from idleness, possibly also from laziness. To save oneself trouble.

Agatha Christie

In reality, serendipity accounts for 1 percent of the blessings we receive in life, work and love. The other 99 per cent is due to our efforts.

Peter McWilliams

A man is not idle because he is absorbed in thought. There is a visible labour and there is an invisible labour.

Victor Hugo

Slump, and the world slumps with you. Push, and you push alone.

Laurence J. Peter

The big secret in life is that there is no big secret. Whatever your goal, you can get there if you're willing to work.

Oprah Winfrey

The day will happen whether or not you get up.

John Ciardi

Idleness is not doing nothing. Idleness is being free to do anything.

Floyd Dell

I have found it advisable not to give too much heed to what people say when I am trying to accomplish something of consequence. Invariably they proclaim it can't be done. I deem that the very best time to make the effort.

Calvin Coolidge

It does not matter how slowly you go so long as you do not stop.

Confucius

The more I practise, the luckier I get.

Gary Player

People are not lazy. They simply have impotent goals – that is, goals that do not inspire them.

Tony Robbins

People who are always making allowances for themselves soon go bankrupt.

Mary Pettibone Poole

There is no sudden leap into the stratosphere. There is only advancing step by step, slowly and tortuously, up the pyramid towards your goals.

Ben Stein

You have to run as fast as you can just to stay where you are. If you want to get anywhere, you'll have to run much faster.

Lewis Carroll

Hard work has made it easy. That is my secret. That is why I win.

Nadia Comaneci

A man who dares to waste one hour of time has not discovered the value of life.

Charles Darwin

Reputation
and character

In most of us,
by the age of 30,
the character has set
like plaster and will
never soften again.

William James

Many a man's reputation would not know his character if they met on the street.

Elbert Hubbard

A man with a so-called character is often a simple piece of mechanism; he has often only one point of view for the extremely complicated relationships of life.

August Strindberg

A man's character is his fate.

Heraclitus

If you don't like my opinion of you, you can always improve.

Ashleigh Brilliant

Character is what God and the angels know of us; reputation is what men and women think of us.

Horace Mann

Self-esteem is the reputation we acquire with ourselves.

Nathaniel Branden

Ability may get you to the top,
but it takes character to keep you there.

John Wooden

As I grow older, I pay
less attention to what
men say. I just watch
what they do.

Andrew Carnegie

Until you've lost your reputation, you never realise what a burden it was.

Margaret Mitchell

Each man is afraid of his neighbour's disapproval – a thing which, to the general run of the human race, is more dreaded than wolves and death.

Mark Twain

I am not in this world to live up to other people's expectations, nor do I feel that the world must live up to mine.

Fritz Perls

Time goes by: reputation increases, ability declines.

Dag Hammarskjöld

When we are young we generally estimate an opinion by the size of the person that holds it, but later we find that is an uncertain rule, for we realise that there are times when a hornet's opinion disturbs us more than an emperor's.

Mark Twain

To avoid criticism,
do nothing,
say nothing
and be nothing.

Elbert Hubbard

Applause is the spur of noble minds, the end and aim of weak ones.

Edmund Burke

Most men are bad.

Bias of Priene

We judge ourselves by what we feel capable of doing, while others judge us by what we have already done.

Henry Wadsworth Longfellow

The less you value and accept yourself the more likely you are to be harsh in your judgments of yourself and others.

Dorothy Rowe

Every man in the world is better than someone else. And not as good as someone else.

William Saroyan

I'm the girl who lost her reputation and never missed it.

Mae West

You probably wouldn't worry about what people think of you if you could know how seldom they do.

Olin Miller

Though I've belted you and flayed you,
By the livin' Gawd that made you,
You're a better man than I am, Gunga Din!

Rudyard Kipling

You can tell a lot about a fellow's character by his way of eating jellybeans.

Ronald Reagan

KARL MARX

SIGMUND FREUD

MOTHER TERESA

RICHARD BRANSON

F. SCOTT FITZGERALD

ERNEST HEMINGWAY

P.G.

CHARLES DE GAULLE

W. SOMERSET MAUGHAM

PETER USTINOV

MICHELANGELO

EDDIE IZZARD

ALBERT CAMUS

ALAN BENNETT

GEORGE BERNARD

JOAN RIVERS

JONATHAN SWIFT

QUENTIN CRISP

W.H. AUDEN

MUHAMMAD ALI

DOLLY PARTON

JEAN-PAUL SARTRE

GEORGE ORWELL

WALT DISNEY

DOUGLAS ADAMS

JOHN F. KENNEDY

DOROTHY PARKER

ALBERT EINSTEIN

NELSON MANDELA

FRANK ZAPPA

OSCAR WILDE

MARGARET THATCHER

PABLO PICASSO **AESOP**

MARK TWAIN

WODEHOUSE BILL CLINTON

LEO TOLSTOY

ORSON WELLES

ISAAC ASIMOV

BUDDHA GROUCHO MARX

VIRGINIA WOOLF

JANE AUSTEN SAMUEL PEPYS

W.C. FIELDS MARILYN MONROE

SHAW **MAE WEST**

BERTRAND RUSSELL

MODERN LIFE

Business and commerce

Teamwork is always essential in a sales force. That way you always have someone to blame.

Donald Trump

Finance is the art of passing currency from hand to hand until it finally disappears.

Robert W. Sarnoff

Executives are like joggers. If you stop a jogger, he goes on running on the spot. If you drag an executive away from his business, he goes on running on the spot, pawing the ground, talking business. He never stops hurtling onwards, making decisions and executing them.

Jean Baudrillard

No one has a greater asset for his business than a man's pride in his work.

Hosea Ballou

Dressing up is inevitably a substitute for good ideas. It is no coincidence that technically inept business types are known as 'suits'.

Paul Graham

Most projects start out slowly and then sort of taper off.

Norman R. Augustine

Never invest in a business you cannot understand.

Warren Buffet

Business opportunities are like buses, there's always another one coming.

Richard Branson

Incompetents invariably make trouble for people other than themselves.

Larry McMurtry

In the modern world of business, it is useless to be a creative original thinker unless you can also sell what you create. Management cannot be expected to recognise a good idea unless it is presented to them by a good salesman.

David Ogilvy

You can't fake quality any more than you can fake a good meal.

William S. Burroughs

A molehill man is a pseudo-busy executive who comes to work at 9am and finds a molehill on his desk. He has until 5pm to make this molehill into a mountain. An accomplished molehill man will often have his mountain finished before lunch.

Fred Allen

The secret of successful managing is to keep the five guys who hate you away from the four guys who haven't made up their minds.

Casey Stengel

Underpromise; overdeliver.

Tom Peters

There are two essential rules to management. One, the customer is always right; and two, they must be punished for their arrogance.

Scott Adams

Nothing is illegal if one hundred businessmen decide to do it.
Andrew Young

When business is bad, always start weeding out at the top.
Graham Day

Build a **better mousetrap** and the world will beat **a path** to your door.

Ralph Waldo Emerson

A professional is a man who can do his job when he doesn't feel like it; an amateur is one who can't do his job even when he does feel like it.

James Agate

The salary of the chief executive of a large corporation is not a market award for achievement. It is frequently in the nature of a warm personal gesture by the individual to himself.

J.K. Galbraith

One of the symptoms of approaching nervous breakdown is the belief that one's work is terribly important. If I were a medical man I would prescribe a holiday to every patient who believed their work to be important.

Bertrand Russell

A big shot is a little shot who kept shooting.
Louis Safian

Money money money

Poverty keeps together
more homes than it
breaks up.

Saki

My worst fault is my belief that if you put bills unopened
behind a picture frame, there is no need to pay them.

Hermione Gingold

Money is a good thing to have. It frees you from doing
things you dislike. Since I dislike doing practically
everthing, that's why I like it so much.

Groucho Marx

Never talk about money to people who have much more
or less of it than you.

Katharine Whitehorn

When somebody says 'It ain't the money but the principle
of the thing,' it's the money.

Elbert Hubbard

Gentlemen prefer bonds.

Andrew Mellon

Those who have money think that the most important
thing in the world is love. The poor know it is money.

Gerald Brenan

When I was young I used to think that wealth and power
could bring me happiness – I was right.

Gahan Wilson

Every time you spend money, you're casting a vote for
the kind of world you want.

Anna Lappé

Much ingenuity with a little money
is vastly more profitable and amusing
than much money without ingenuity.

Arnold Bennett

Why pay a dollar for
a bookmark? Why not
use the dollar for a
bookmark?

Steven Spielberg

Inflation is bringing us true democracy. For the first time in history, luxuries and necessities are selling at the same price.
Robert Orben

Money, it turned out, was exactly like sex. You thought of nothing else if you didn't have it and thought of other things if you did.
James Baldwin

You should go on living just to annoy those who are paying your annuities.
Voltaire

Money speaks sense in a language all nations understand.
Aphra Behn

A wise man should have money in his head, but not in his heart.
Jonathan Swift

In spite of the cost of living, it's still popular.
Laurence J. Peter

The darkest hour in any man's life is when he sits down to plan how to get money without earning it.
Horace Greeley

It's diamonds in your pockets one week, macaroni and cheese the next.
Jolene Blalock

Money is a singular thing. It ranks with love as man's greatest source of joy. And with death as his greatest source of anxiety. Over all history it has oppressed nearly all people in one of two ways: either it has been abundant and very unreliable, or reliable and very scarce.
J.K. Galbraith

There is only one class in the community that thinks more about money than the rich, and that is the poor.
Oscar Wilde

Why is there so much month left at the end of the money?
John Barrymore

Whoever said money can't buy happiness simply didn't know where to go shopping.
Bo Derek

I'd like to live like a poor man – only with lots of money.
Pablo Picasso

Rich and poor

All heiresses are beautiful.

John Dryden

The trouble with being poor is that it takes up all of your time.

Ogden Nash

I've been rich and I've been poor. Believe me, rich is better.

Sophie Tucker

The only thing money gives you is the freedom of not worrying about money.

Johnny Carson

Of all the preposterous assumptions of humanity over humanity, nothing exceeds most of the criticisms made on the habits of the poor by the well-housed, well-warmed and well-fed.

Herman Melville

Some people get so rich they lose all respect for humanity. That's how rich I want to get.

Rita Rudner

When a man tells you that he got rich through hard work, ask him: 'Whose?'

Don Marquis

A rich man's joke is always funny.

Thomas Edward Brown

Though I am grateful for the blessings of wealth, it hasn't changed who I am. My feet are still on the ground. I'm just wearing better shoes.

Oprah Winfrey

What's the quickest way to become a millionaire?
Borrow fivers off everyone you meet.

Richard Branson

The advantage of a classical education is that it enables you
to despise the wealth which it prevents you from achieving.

Russell Green

You cannot sift out the poor from the community.
The poor are indispensable to the rich.

Henry Ward Beecher

Poverty is the parent of revolution and crime.

Aristotle

The easiest way for your children to learn about money
is for you not to have any.

Katharine Whitehorn

Being a millionaire is
a bit like being poor,
but having a hell of
a lot of money.
Griff Rhys Jones

It isn't necessary to be **rich** and **famous** to be
happy. It's only necessary to be **rich.**

Alan Alda

No matter how rich you become, how famous or powerful,
when you die the size of your funeral will still pretty much
depend on the weather.

Michael Pritchard

Poverty is an anomaly to rich people; it is very difficult to
make out why people who want dinner do not ring the bell.

Walter Bagehot

It is pretty hard to tell what does bring happiness;
poverty and wealth have both failed.

Kin Hubbard

If you can count your money, you don't have
a billion dollars.

J. Paul Getty

A large income is the best recipe for happiness
I ever heard of.

Jane Austen

The surest way to
remain poor is to be
an honest man.
Napoleon Bonaparte

Earning a living

A desk is a dangerous place from which to watch the world.

John le Carré

Never continue in a job you don't enjoy. If you're happy in what you're doing, you'll like yourself, you'll have inner peace. And if you have that, along with physical health, you will have had more success than you could possibly have imagined.

Johnny Carson

Getting fired is nature's way of telling you that you had the wrong job in the first place.

Hal Lancaster

All paid jobs absorb and degrade the mind.

Aristotle

Gain a modest reputation for being unreliable and you will never be asked to do a thing.

Paul Theroux

Open your mail over the wastebasket.

Jeff Davidson

Careers, like rockets, don't always take off on time. The trick is to always keep the engine running.

Gary Sinise

The key is not to prioritise what's on your schedule, but to schedule your priorities.

Stephen Covey

Be nice to people on your way up because you meet them on your way down.

Jimmy Durante

All I've **ever wanted** was an honest week's pay for an **honest day's work.**

Steve Martin

You moon the wrong person at an office party and suddenly you're not 'professional' anymore.

Jeff Foxworthy

By working faithfully 8 hours a day, you may get to be a boss and work 12 hours a day.

Robert Frost

Amateur musicians practise until they can get it right; professionals practise until they can't get it wrong.

Anon

What the world really needs is more love and less paperwork.

Pearl Bailey

A memorandum is written not to inform the reader but to protect the writer.

Dean Acheson

The only risk of failure is promotion.

Scott Adams

Getting ahead in a difficult profession requires avid faith in yourself. That is why some people with mediocre talent, but with great inner drive, go much further than people with vastly superior talent.

Sophia Loren

Choose a job you love, and you will never have to work a day in your life.

Confucius

Any task can be completed in only one-third more time than is currently estimated.

Norman R. Augustine

You'll never prove you're too good for a job by not doing your best.

Ethel Merman

Professionals built the Titanic; amateurs built the Ark.

Anon

Few great men would have got past personnel.

Paul Goodman

The longer the title, the less important the job.

George McGovern

Quotations
for **retirement**

You have been working most of your days – time to put away the briefcase or tools and get out the gardening gloves and golf clubs. Along with the carriage clock, flowers and leaving card, here is some wit and wisdom to send you into a happy retirement.

If wrinkles must be written upon our brows, let them not be written upon the heart. The spirit should never grow old.
J.K. Galbraith

Retirement at 65 is ridiculous. When I was 65 I still had pimples.
George Burns

Age is only a number, a cipher for the records. A man can't retire his experience. He must use it.
Bernard Baruch

Musicians don't retire; they stop when there's no more music in them.
Louis Armstrong

Retirement: the transition from Who's Who to Who's He.
Eddie George

My passion strengthens daily to quit political turmoil, and retire into the bosom of my family, the only scene of sincere and pure happiness.
Thomas Jefferson

I'm retired – goodbye tension, hello pension!
Anon

Life begins at retirement.
Anon

And in the end, it's not the years in your life that count. It's the life in your years.
Abraham Lincoln

I will not retire while I still have my legs and my make-up box.
Bette Davis

Cherish all your happy moments: they make a fine cushion for old age.
Christopher Morley

My grandmother started walking 5 miles a day when she was 60. She's 97 now, and we don't know where the hell she is.
Ellen DeGeneres

I'm 61 today,
A year beyond the barrier,
And what was once a Magic Flute
Is now a Water Carrier.
Anon

There's nothing worse than being an ageing young person.
Richard Pryor

It is the secret of the world that all things subsist and do not die, but only retire from sight and afterwards return again.
Ralph Waldo Emerson

When a man fell into his anecdotage, it was a sign for him to retire from the world.
Benjamin Disraeli

To retire to the monastery, or the woods, or the sea, is to escape from the sharp suggestions that spur on ambition.
Charles Horton Cooley

The trouble with retirement is that you never get a day off.
Abe Lemons

In this country, men seem to live for action as long as they can and sink into apathy when they retire.
Charles Francis Adams

I refuse to admit that I am more than 52, even if that does make my sons illegitimate.
Nancy Astor

The **technological** world

Inanimate objects can be classified scientifically into three major categories: those that don't work, those that break down and those that get lost.

Russell Baker

I get mail; therefore I am.

Scott Adams

The robot is going to lose. Not by much. But when the final score is tallied, flesh and blood is going to beat the damn monster.

Adam Smith

Never trust a computer you can't throw out a window.

Steve Wozniak

My favorite thing about the internet is that you get to go into the private world of real creeps without having to smell them.

Penn Jillette

Men have become the tools of their tools.

Henry David Thoreau

One machine can do the work of 50 ordinary men. No machine can do the work of one extraordinary man.

Elbert Hubbard

To invent, you need a good imagination and **a pile of junk.**

Thomas Alva Edison

The future is here. It's just not widely distributed yet.

William Gibson

I think computer viruses should count as life. I think it says something about human nature that the only form of life we have created so far is purely destructive. We've created life in our own image.

Stephen Hawking

We've heard that a million monkeys at a million keyboards could produce the complete works of Shakespeare. Now, thanks to the internet, we know that is not true.

Robert Wilensky

To err is human – and to blame it on a computer is even more so.

Robert Orben

A common mistake that people make when trying to design something completely foolproof is to underestimate the ingenuity of complete fools.

Douglas Adams

Engineers like to solve problems. If there are no problems handily available, they will create their own problems.

Scott Adams

We are more ready to try the untried when what we do is inconsequential. Hence the fact that many inventions had their birth as toys.

Eric Hoffer

The best way to predict the future is to invent it.

Alan Kay

A computer lets you make more mistakes faster than any invention in human history – with the possible exceptions of handguns and tequila.

Mitch Ratliffe

The first rule of intelligent tinkering is to save all the parts.

Paul Ehrlich

Humanity is acquiring all the right technology for all the wrong reasons.

R. Buckminster Fuller

The most likely way for the world to be destroyed, most experts agree, is by accident. That's where we come in; we're computer professionals. We cause accidents.

Nathaniel Borenstein

Our scientific power has outrun our spiritual power. We have guided missiles and misguided men.

Martin Luther King, Jnr

It pays to advertise

Advertising is the rattling of a stick inside a swill-bucket.

George Orwell

It is far easier to write ten passably effective sonnets, good enough to take in the not too enquiring critic, than one effective advertisement that will take in a few thousand of the uncritical buying public.

Aldous Huxley

Society drives people crazy with lust and calls it advertising.

John Lahr

Advertising may be described as the science of arresting human intelligence long enough to get money from it.

Stephen Leacock

Doing business without advertising is like winking at a girl in the dark. You know what you are doing, but nobody else does.

Edgar Howe

You can tell the ideals of a nation by its advertisements.

Norman Douglas

We grew up founding our dreams on the infinite promise of American advertising. I still believe that one can learn to play the piano by mail and that mud will give you a perfect complexion.

Zelda Fitzgerald

Advertising isn't a science. It's persuasion. And persuasion is an art.

William Bernbach

Half the money I spend on advertising is wasted; the trouble is I don't know which half.

John Wanamaker

I have learned that any fool can write a bad ad, but that it takes a real genius to keep his hands off a good one.

Leo Burnett

Advertising is the greatest art form of the 20th century.

Marshall McLuhan

The philosophy behind much advertising is based on the old observation that every man is really two men – the man he is and the man he wants to be.

William Feather

Advertising is a valuable economic factor because it is the cheapest way of selling goods, particularly if the goods are worthless.

Sinclair Lewis

A great ad campaign will make a bad product fail faster. It will get more people to know it's bad.

William Bernbach

Living in an age of advertisement, we are perpetually disillusioned. The perfect life is spread before us every day, but it changes and withers at a touch.

J.B. Priestley

Promise, large promise, is the soul of an advertisement.

Samuel Johnson

Advertising is the modern substitute for argument; its function is to make the worse appear the better.

George Santayana

What is the difference between unethical and ethical advertising? Unethical advertising uses falsehoods to deceive the public; ethical advertising uses truth to deceive the public.

Vilhjalmur Stefansson

Advertisers are the interpreters of our dreams. Like the movies, they infect the routine futility of our days with purposeful adventure. Their weapons are our weaknesses: fear, ambition, illness, pride, selfishness, desire, ignorance. And these weapons must be kept as bright as a sword.

E.B. White

Few people at the beginning of the 19th century needed an adman to tell them what they wanted.

J.K. Galbraith

Advertising is a racket, like the movies and the brokerage business. You cannot be honest without admitting that its constructive contribution to humanity is exactly minus zero.

F. Scott Fitzgerald

> Advertising has annihilated the power of the most powerful adjectives.
> **Paul Valéry**

Crime and punishment

The degree of civilisation in a society can be judged by entering its prisons.

Fedor Dostoevsky

No punishment has ever possessed enough power of deterrence to prevent the commission of crimes.

Hannah Arendt

Behind every great fortune there is a crime.

Honoré de Balzac

Abscond: to 'move in a mysterious way', commonly with the property of another.

Ambrose Bierce

Sometimes it's an easy option for a youngster to go into prison for a short time and sit on his bed in his cell doing nothing.

Lord Woolf

I have come to regard the law courts not as cathedrals but casinos.

Richard Ingrams

The fear of burglars is not only the fear of being robbed, but also the fear of a sudden and unexpected clutch out of the darkness.

Elias Canetti

A thief believes everybody steals.

Edward W. Howe

Squeeze human nature into the strait jacket of criminal justice and crime will appear.

Karl Kraus

Obviously crime pays, or there'd be no crime.

G. Gordon Liddy

Crime is terribly revealing. Try and vary your methods as you will, your tastes, your habits, your attitude of mind, and your soul is revealed by your actions.

Agatha Christie

Everybody has a little bit of Watergate in him.

Billy Graham

It is better that ten guilty escape than one innocent suffer.

William Blackstone

The truth of the matter is that muggers are very interesting people.

Michael Winner

Crime is only a left-handed form of human endeavour.

John Huston

The lyricism of marginality may find inspiration in the image of the 'outlaw', the great social nomad, who prowls on the fringes of a docile, frightened order.

Michel Foucault

The road to Easy Street goes through the sewer.

John Madden

We may not all break the Ten Commandments, but we are certainly all capable of it. Within us lurks the breaker of all laws, ready to spring out at the first real opportunity.

Isadora Duncan

The guilty think all talk is of themselves.

Geoffrey Chaucer

An eye for an eye makes the whole world blind.

Mahatma Gandhi

Like art and politics, gangsterism is a very important avenue of assimilation into society.

E.L. Doctorow

The **number one rule** of thieves is that **nothing** is too small to steal.

Jimmy Breslin

Went out to Charing Cross, to see Major-General Harrison hanged, drawn; and quartered; which was done there, he looking as cheerful as any man could do in that condition.

Samuel Pepys

Crime and bad lives are the measure of a state's failure. All crime in the end is the crime of the community.

H.G. Wells

They say, 'Guns don't kill people, people kill people.' Well, I think the gun helps. If you just stood there and yelled 'BANG', I don't think you'd kill too many people.

Eddie Izzard

Style and fashion

As martyrs burn for Christ, so ladies freeze for fashion.

C.H. Spurgeon

I hold that gentleman to be the best dressed whose dress no one observes.

Anthony Trollope

We seem to believe it is possible to ward off death by following rules of good grooming.

Don DeLillo

It doesn't matter one damn bit whether fashion is art or not. You don't question whether an incredible chef is an artist or not – his cakes are delicious and that's all that matters. Fashion is there to serve a purpose.

Sonia Rykiel

For a brief moment everything seems better, when you've got a new dress that you look good in.

Alexandra Shulman

I love clothes. If I can have any impact, I want women to feel good about themselves and have fun with fashion.

Michelle Obama

In Los Angeles everyone has perfect teeth. It's crocodile land.

Gwyneth Paltrow

The most important item in a woman's wardrobe is a good pair of trousers.

Nicole Farhi

Do not read **beauty magazines.** They only make you **feel ugly.**

Mary Schmich

The most important item in a woman's wardrobe is a suit.

Paul Smith

Women thrive on novelty and are easy meat for the commerce of fashion. Men prefer old pipes and torn jackets.

Anthony Burgess

I think I'm vaguely blonde. To be perfectly frank, I don't know.

Cate Blanchett

Fashion is what you adopt when you don't know who you are.

Quentin Crisp

Luxury must be comfortable, otherwise it is not luxury.

Coco Chanel

I base my fashion taste on what doesn't itch.

Gilda Radner

Women are most fascinating between the ages of 35 and 40 after they have won a few races and know how to pace themselves. Since few women ever pass 40, maximum fascination can continue indefinitely.

Christian Dior

I can't take a well-tanned person seriously.

Cleveland Amory

Art produces ugly things which frequently become more beautiful with time. Fashion, on the other hand, produces beautiful things which always become ugly with time.

Jean Cocteau

Fashion can be bought. Style one must possess.

Edna Woolman Chase

Put even the plainest woman into a beautiful dress and unconsciously she will try to live up to it.

Lucie Duff-Gordon

The fashion wears out more apparel than the man.

William Shakespeare

Every generation laughs at the old fashions but religiously follows the new.

Henry David Thoreau

Where lipstick is concerned, the important thing is not colour, but to accept God's final word on where your lips end.

Jerry Seinfeld

You have no idea how much it costs to look this cheap.

Dolly Parton

I think that the most important thing a woman can have – next to talent, of course – is her hairdresser.

Joan Crawford

The media are the message

Have you ever observed that we pay much more attention to a wise passage when it is quoted than when we read it in the original author?

Philip G. Hamerton

The new electronic independence recreates the world in the image of a global village.

Marshall McLuhan

If we had 3 million exhibitionists and only one voyeur, nobody could make any money.

Albert Brooks

A public-opinion poll is no substitute for thought.

Warren Buffett

It's amazing that the amount of news that happens in the world every day always just exactly fits the newspaper.

Jerry Seinfeld

Trying to determine what is going on in the world by reading newspapers is like trying to tell the time by watching the second hand of a clock.

Ben Hecht

Journalism largely consists of saying 'Lord Jones is dead' to people who never knew that Lord Jones was alive.

G.K. Chesterton

I'm all in favour of keeping dangerous weapons out of the hands of fools. Let's start with typewriters.

Frank Lloyd Wright

When a dog bites a man, that is not news … but if a man bites a dog, that is news.

John B. Bogart

A good newspaper, I suppose, is a nation talking to itself.

Arthur Miller

A newspaper is lumber made malleable. It is ink made into words and pictures. It is conceived, born, grows up and dies of old age in a day.

Jim Bishop

What the mass media offers is not popular art, but entertainment which is intended to be consumed like food, forgotten, and replaced by a new dish.

W.H. Auden

I take the view, and always have, that if you cannot say what you are going to say in 20 minutes you ought to go away and write a book about it.

Lord Brabazon

Four hostile newspapers are more to be feared than a thousand bayonets.

Napoleon Bonaparte

I read the newspapers avidly. It is my one form of continuous fiction.

Aneurin Bevan

A free press can, of course, be good or bad, but, most certainly without freedom, the press will never be anything but bad.

Albert Camus

Never pick a fight with people who buy ink by the barrel.
Bill Clinton

The **pen is mightier than the sword**, and considerably easier to **write** with.

Marty Feldman

You can never get all the facts from just one newspaper, and unless you have all the facts, you cannot make proper judgments about what is going on.

Harry S Truman

Editor: a person employed by a newspaper, whose business it is to separate the wheat from the chaff, and to see that the chaff is printed.

Elbert Hubbard

A journalist is a person who has mistaken his calling.

Otto von Bismarck

Fame and celebrity

You're not a star until they can spell your name in Karachi.
Humphrey Bogart

Being in the public eye is like being the lady with the moustache at the circus. You're a curiosity, and you will never stop being one.

Christine Keeler

Blessed are the famous, for they will enjoy the praise of men.

George Carey

It's a lot easier to be famous than to be a decent person.

Liza Tarbuck

Celebrity is bestial. It is the worst type of karma because of the huge solitude it brings. You're like a gazelle that finds itself straying from the flock. And soon your path is cut off by lions.

Brad Pitt

Fame is like a river, that beareth up things light and swollen, and drowns things weighty and solid.

Francis Bacon

It's better to be known by six people for something you're proud of than by 60 million for something you're not.

Albert Brooks

There is no such thing as bad publicity except your own obituary.

Brendan Behan

Now when I bore people at a party they think it's their fault.

Henry Kissinger

Once you're dead you're made for life.

Jimi Hendrix

The only reason I'm in Hollywood is that I don't have the moral courage to refuse the money.

Marlon Brando

Glamour is what I sell. It's my stock in trade.

Marlene Dietrich

I have been very happy, very rich, very beautiful, much adulated, very famous and very unhappy.

Brigitte Bardot

A celebrity is a person who works hard all his life to become well known, then wears dark glasses to avoid being recognised.

Fred Allen

In the future everybody will be world famous for 15 minutes.

Andy Warhol

Actors have bodyguards and entourages not because anybody wants to hurt them – who would want to hurt an actor? – but because they want to get recognised. God forbid someone doesn't recognise them.

James Caan

Hollywood is a place where a man can get stabbed in the back while climbing a ladder.

William Faulkner

Fame is only good for one thing – they will cash your cheque in a small town.

Truman Capote

Fame is a fickle food upon a shifting plate.

Emily Dickinson

A celebrity is one who is known to many persons he is glad he doesn't know.

H.L. Mencken

Fame is like a shaved pig with a greased tail, and it is only after it has slipped through the hands of some thousands, that some fellow, by mere chance, holds on to it!

Davy Crockett

If you want a place in the sun, you've got to expect a few blisters.
Abigail Van Buren

Fame is like a big piece of meringue – it's beautiful and you keep eating it, but it doesn't really fill you up.
Pierce Brosnan

Mark Twain

CHRONICLER OF A BRAVE NEW AMERICA

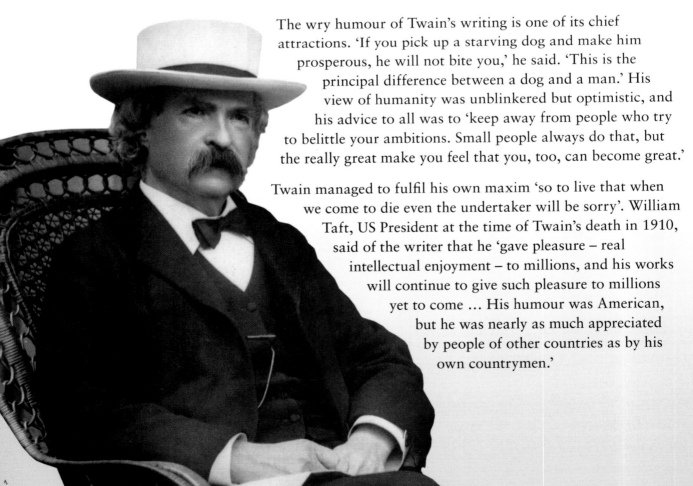

Mark Twain, born Samuel Langhorne Clemens in the midwestern state of Missouri in 1835, is the revered godfather of American letters. Through his journalism, travel writing and fiction he created exotic landscape pictures of the United States in its most dynamic phase – as the country grew and spread westward. His *Adventures of Huckleberry Finn* (1885), set on the broad, slow-flowing Mississippi River, was decribed by Ernest Hemingway as the genesis for 'all modern American literature'.

The wry humour of Twain's writing is one of its chief attractions. 'If you pick up a starving dog and make him prosperous, he will not bite you,' he said. 'This is the principal difference between a dog and a man.' His view of humanity was unblinkered but optimistic, and his advice to all was to 'keep away from people who try to belittle your ambitions. Small people always do that, but the really great make you feel that you, too, can become great.'

Twain managed to fulfil his own maxim 'so to live that when we come to die even the undertaker will be sorry'. William Taft, US President at the time of Twain's death in 1910, said of the writer that he 'gave pleasure – real intellectual enjoyment – to millions, and his works will continue to give such pleasure to millions yet to come … His humour was American, but he was nearly as much appreciated by people of other countries as by his own countrymen.'

✳

Cold! If the thermometer had been an inch longer
we'd all have frozen to death.

✳

I don't give a damn for a man that can only spell a word one way.

✳

Total abstinence is so excellent a thing that it cannot be carried
to too great an extent. In my passion for it I even carry it so far
as to totally abstain from total abstinence itself.

✳

The best way to cheer yourself up is to try to cheer somebody else up.

✳

A classic is something that everybody wants
to have read and nobody wants to read.

✳

When you catch an adjective, kill it. No, I don't mean utterly, but kill
most of them – then the rest will be valuable. They weaken when
they are close together. They give strength when they are wide apart.

✳

Cauliflower is nothing but cabbage with a college education.

✳

Each man is afraid of his neighbour's disapproval –
a thing which, to the general run of the human race,
is more dreaded than wolves and death.

✳

Supposing is good, but finding out is better.

✳

One of the most striking differences between a cat
and a lie is that a cat has only nine lives.

Work and vocation

> I work until beer o'clock.
> **Stephen King**

It's true hard work never killed anybody, but I figure, why take the chance?

Ronald Reagan

It is easier to do a job right than to explain why you didn't.

Martin Van Buren

The more I want to get something done, the less I call it work.

Richard Bach

Hard work spotlights the character of people: some turn up their sleeves, some turn up their noses, and some don't turn up at all.

Sam Ewing

It's a job that's never started that takes the longest to finish.

J.R.R. Tolkien

I have long been of the opinion that if work were such a splendid thing the rich would have kept more of it for themselves.

Bruce Grocott

Anything not worth doing is worth not doing well. Think about it.

Elias Schwartz

Do the **hard jobs** first. The **easy jobs** will take care of themselves.

Dale Carnegie

Be true to your work, your word, and your friend.

Henry David Thoreau

If I had 8 hours to chop down a tree, I'd spend 6 hours sharpening my axe.

Abraham Lincoln

What we really want to do is what we are really meant to do. When we do what we are meant to do, money comes to us, doors open for us, we feel useful, and the work we do feels like play to us.

Julia Cameron

Work expands so as to fill the time available for its completion.

C. Northcote Parkinson

The key is to figure out what you want out of life, not what you want out of your career.

Goldie Hawn

There is time for work. And time for love. That leaves no other time.

Coco Chanel

I do not pray for a lighter load, but for a stronger back.

Phillips Brooks

People forget how fast you did a job, but they remember how well you did it.

Howard Newton

I like work: it fascinates me. I can sit and look at it for hours.

Jerome K. Jerome

Nothing is particularly hard if you divide it into small jobs.

Henry Ford

In work the greatest satisfaction lies – the satisfaction of stretching yourself, using your abilities and making them expand, and knowing that you have accomplished something that could have been done only by you using your unique apparatus. This is really the centre of life, and those who never orientate themselves in this direction are missing more than they ever know.

Kenneth Allsop

Get happiness out of your work or you may never know what happiness is.

Elbert Hubbard

The only way to enjoy life is to work. Work is much more fun than fun.

Noël Coward

Follow my leader

Don't tell people how to do things. Tell them what to do and let them surprise you with their results.
George S. Patton

Eagles don't flock –
you have to find them
one at a time.
H. Ross Perot

I believe managing is like holding a dove in your hand. If you hold it too tightly you kill it, but if you hold it too loosely, you lose it.

Tommy Lasorda

The very essence of leadership is that you have to have vision. You can't blow an uncertain trumpet.

Theodore Hesburgh

The most important quality in a leader is that of being acknowledged as such. All leaders whose fitness is questioned are clearly lacking in force.

André Maurois

The question 'Who ought to be boss?' is like asking 'Who ought to be the tenor in the quartet?' Obviously, the man who can sing tenor.

Henry Ford

Leadership is intangible, and therefore no weapon ever designed can replace it.

Omar N. Bradley

Few things can help an individual more than to place responsibility on him, and to let him know that you trust him.

Booker T. Washington

Three billion people on the face of the earth go to bed hungry every night, but 4 billion people go to bed every night hungry for a simple word of encouragement and recognition.

Cavett Robert

A good leader can't get too far ahead of his followers.

Franklin D. Roosevelt

Motivation is everything. You can do the work of two people, but you can't be two people. Instead, you have to inspire the next guy down the line and get him to inspire his people.

Lee Iacocca

The way to get things done is not to mind who gets the credit for doing them.

Benjamin Jowett

The view only changes for the lead dog.

Norman O. Brown

Example is not the main thing in influencing others. It is the only thing.

Albert Schweitzer

The great leaders are like the best conductors – they reach beyond the notes to reach the magic in the players.

Blaine Lee

Without initiative, leaders are simply workers in leadership positions.

Bo Bennett

I am personally convinced that one person can be a change catalyst, a 'transformer' in any situation, any organisation. Such an individual is yeast that can leaven an entire loaf. It requires vision, initiative, patience, respect, persistence, courage, and faith to be a transforming leader.

Stephen Covey

The people to fear are not those who disagree with you, but those who disagree with you and are too cowardly to let you know.

Napoleon Bonaparte

No man will make a great leader who wants to do it all himself or get all the credit for doing it.

Andrew Carnegie

The employer generally gets the employees he deserves.
J. Paul Getty

Problems and solutions

Each success only buys an admission ticket to a more difficult problem.

Henry Kissinger

I have yet to see any problem, however complicated, which, when you looked at it in the right way, did not become still more complicated.

Poul Anderson

The best way to escape from a problem is to solve it.

Alan Saporta

If a problem has no solution, it may not be a problem, but a fact – not to be solved, but to be coped with over time.

Shimon Peres

Every problem has a gift for you in its hands.

Richard Bach

Our problems are man-made, therefore they may be solved by man. And man can be as big as he wants. No problem of human destiny is beyond human beings.

John F. Kennedy

If the only tool you have is a hammer, you tend to see every problem as a nail.

Abraham Maslow

Any solution to a problem changes the problem.

Robert Wood Johnson

It is characteristic of all deep human problems that they are not to be approached without some humour and some bewilderment.

Freeman Dyson

The real problem is what to do with the problem-solvers after the problems are solved.

Gay Talese

There's more than one way to look at a problem, and they all may be right.

H. Norman Schwarzkopf

No problem is too big to run away from.

Charles M. Schulz

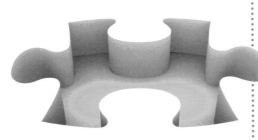

If you find a good solution and become attached to it, the solution may become your next problem.

Robert Anthony

Four-fifths of all our troubles would disappear, if we would only sit down and keep still.

Calvin Coolidge

The problem is not that there are problems. The problem is expecting otherwise and thinking that having problems is a problem.

Theodore Rubin

Don't get involved in partial problems, but always take flight to where there is a free view over the whole single great problem, even if this view is still not a clear one.

Ludwig Wittgenstein

Again and again, the impossible problem is solved when we see that the problem is only a tough decision waiting to be made.

Robert Schuller

The greatest challenge to any thinker is stating the problem in a way that will allow a solution.

Bertrand Russell

The colour of the cat doesn't matter so long as it catches the mice.

Deng Xiaoping

When we ask for **advice**, we are usually looking for an **accomplice.**

Saul Bellow

It isn't that they can't see the solution. It is that they can't see the problem.

G.K. Chesterton

Somehow we should learn to know that our problems are our most precious possessions. They are the raw materials of our salvation: no problem, no redemption.

Laurens van der Post

Probable impossibilities are to be preferred to improbable possibilities.

Aristotle

Success and failure

Formula for success:
rise early, work
hard, strike oil.

J. Paul Getty

There is nobody more boring than the undefeated.
Any great, long career has at least one flame-out in it.

Tina Brown

When people say 'I'll let you know,' you know.

Laurence J. Peter

A thinker sees his own actions as experiments and questions
– as attempts to find out something. Success and failure are
for him answers above all.

Friedrich Nietzsche

I couldn't wait for success, so I went ahead
without it.

Jonathan Winters

All the rudiments of success in life can be
found in ironing a pair of trousers.

Chris Eubank

Before anything else, preparation is the key
to success.

Alexander Graham Bell

Success is how high you bounce when you
hit bottom.

George S. Patton

The only place where success comes before
work is in a dictionary.

Vidal Sassoon

*A man is a success if he gets up
in the morning and goes to bed
at night and in between does
what he wants to do.*

Bob Dylan

A man can fail many times, but he isn't a failure until he begins to blame somebody else.

John Burroughs

A minute's success pays the failure of years.

Robert Browning

Failure is unimportant. It takes courage to make a fool of yourself.

Charlie Chaplin

If you know you are going to fail, then fail gloriously.

Cate Blanchett

My mother drew a distinction between achievement and success. She said that 'achievement is the knowledge that you have studied and worked hard and done the best that is in you. Success is being praised by others, and that's nice, too, but not as important or satisfying. Always aim for achievement and forget about success.'

Helen Hayes

If at first you don't succeed, failure may be your style.

Quentin Crisp

Ninety-nine per cent of the failures come from people who have the habit of making excuses.

George Washington Carver

> The penalty for success is to be bored by the people who used to snub you.
>
> **Nancy Astor**

The **greatest glory** in living lies not in **never falling**, but in rising every time **we fall**.

Nelson Mandela

I can accept failure, but I can't accept not trying.

Michael Jordan

Success is the sum of small efforts – repeated day in and day out.

Robert Collier

Many of life's failures are people who did not realise how close they were to success when they gave up.

Thomas Alva Edison

Risk and adventure

To play it safe is not to play.

Robert Altman

People who go to the polar regions are statistically less likely to die than salesmen who drive on motorways in England.

Ranulph Fiennes

There are two kinds of adventurers: those who go truly hoping to find adventure and those who go secretly hoping they won't.

William Least Heat-Moon

Do not go where the path may lead, go instead where there is no path and leave a trail.

Ralph Waldo Emerson

Our lives improve only when we take chances – and the first and most difficult risk we can take is to be honest with ourselves.

Walter Anderson

The way of the pioneer is always rough.

Harvey S. Firestone

Be daring, be different, be impractical, be anything that will assert integrity of purpose and imaginative vision against the play-it-safers, the creatures of the commonplace, the slaves of the ordinary.

Cecil Beaton

If we do not find anything very pleasant, at least we shall find something new.

Voltaire

Risk comes from not knowing what you're doing.

Warren Buffett

Soar, eat ether, see what has never been seen; depart, be lost, but climb.

Edna St Vincent Millay

Only those who dare to fail greatly can ever achieve greatly.

Robert F. Kennedy

You can't help someone get up a hill without getting closer to the top yourself.

H. Norman Schwarzkopf

People who don't take risks generally make about two big mistakes a year. People who do take risks generally make about two big mistakes a year.

Peter F. Drucker

If the highest aim of a captain were to preserve his ship, he would keep it in port forever.

St Thomas Aquinas

The test of an adventure is that when you're in the middle of it you say to yourself 'Oh, now I've got myself into an awful mess; I wish I were sitting quietly at home'.

Thornton Wilder

Either you decide to stay in the shallow end of the pool or you go out in the ocean.

Christopher Reeve

An adventure is only an inconvenience rightly considered. An inconvenience is only an adventure wrongly considered.

G.K. Chesterton

The big question is whether you are going to be able to say a hearty yes to your adventure.

Joseph Campbell

In skating over thin ice our safety is in our speed.

Ralph Waldo Emerson

Risk! Risk anything! Care no more for the opinions of others, for those voices. Do the hardest thing on earth for you. Act for yourself. Face the truth.

Katherine Mansfield

A little tumult now and then is an agreeable quickener of sensation; such as a revolution, a battle, or an adventure of any lively description.

Lord Byron

We took risks, we knew we took them; things have come out against us, and therefore we have no cause for complaint.

Robert Falcon Scott

Nothing in life is so exhilarating as to be shot at without result.
Winston Churchill

KARL MARX

SIGMUND FREUD

MOTHER TERESA

RICHARD BRANSON

F. SCOTT FITZGERALD

ERNEST HEMINGWAY

P.G.

CHARLES DE GAULLE

W. SOMERSET MAUGHAM

PETER USTINOV

MICHELANGELO

EDDIE IZZARD

ALBERT CAMUS

ALAN BENNETT

GEORGE BERNARD

JOAN RIVERS

JONATHAN SWIFT

QUENTIN CRISP

W.H. AUDEN

MUHAMMAD ALI

DOLLY PARTON

JEAN-PAUL SARTRE

GEORGE ORWELL

WALT DISNEY

DOUGLAS ADAMS

JOHN F. KENNEDY

DOROTHY PARKER

ALBERT EINSTEIN

NELSON MANDELA

FRANK ZAPPA

OSCAR WILDE

MARGARET THATCHER

PABLO PICASSO AESOP

MARK TWAIN

LEO TOLSTOY

ORSON WELLES

ISAAC ASIMOV

BUDDHA GROUCHO MARX

VODEHOUSE BILL CLINTON VIRGINIA WOOLF

JANE AUSTEN SAMUEL PEPYS

W.C. FIELDS MARILYN MONROE

SHAW MAE WEST

BERTRAND RUSSELL

NATIONS AND POLITICS

The **powers** that be

I shall be an autocrat; that's my trade. And the good Lord will forgive me; that's his.

Catherine the Great

The worst thing in this world, next to anarchy, is government.

Henry Ward Beecher

You will find that the State is the kind of organisation which, though it does big things badly, does small things badly, too.

J.K. Galbraith

Being President is like running a cemetery: you've got a lot of people under you and nobody's listening.

Bill Clinton

The government solution to any problem is usually at least as bad as the problem.

Milton Friedman

So long as men worship the Caesars and Napoleons, Caesars and Napoleons will duly arise and make them miserable.

Aldous Huxley

Great leaders are almost always great simplifiers, who can cut through argument, debate and doubt, to offer a solution everybody can understand.

Colin Powell

The art of leadership is saying no, not yes. It is very easy to say yes.

Tony Blair

A friend in power is a friend lost.

Henry Brooks Adams

The politician who never made a mistake never made a decision.

John Major

I am sometimes a fox and sometimes a lion. The whole secret of government lies in knowing when to be the one or the other.

Napoleon Bonaparte

Render therefore unto Caesar the things that are
Caesar's; and unto God the things that are God's.

The Bible (Gospel of Matthew)

Government always finds a need for whatever money it gets.

Ronald Reagan

A government is the only known vessel that leaks
from the top.

James Reston

Those who have been once intoxicated with power, and
have derived any kind of emolument from it, even though
but for one year, never can willingly abandon it. They may
be distressed in the midst of all their power; but they will
never look to anything but power for their relief.

Edmund Burke

We hang the petty thieves, and appoint the great ones
to public office.

Aesop

I have found some of the best reasons I ever had for remaining
at the bottom simply by looking at the men at the top.

Frank Moore Colby

Leaders should never, ever try to look cool. That's for
dictators.

Ben Elton

We have leadership –
there's just no followship.
George E. Danielson

> The price good men
> pay for indifference
> to public affairs is to
> be ruled by evil men.
>
> **Plato**

Govern a great nation as you would
cook a small fish. Do not overdo it.

Lao-Tzu

Governments never learn. Only people learn.

Milton Friedman

Governments are like underpants. They need changing
often, and usually for the same reason.

Italian proverb

Giving money and power to government is like giving
whisky and car keys to teenage boys.

P.J. O'Rourke

Politics and politicians

Politics is for people who are too ugly to get into showbusiness.
Bill Clinton

A diplomat is somebody who can tell you to go to hell and leave you looking forward to the trip.
Alex Salmond

I could never be a politician. I couldn't bear to be right all the time.

Peter Ustinov

If you sack politicians for having affairs, then we are going to have a depleted Commons.

Oona King

I am strongly in favour of common sense, common honesty and common decency. This makes me forever ineligible for public office.

H.L. Mencken

Advice to politicians: always be sincere whether you mean it or not.

Charles Percy

If you are working class, being an MP is the job your parents always wanted for you. It's clean, indoor work and there is no heavy lifting.

Diane Abbott

Every politician is allowed the occasional gaffe, if only to remind the public that they are still human.

Peter Mandelson

It's very hard to be in awe of politicians.

Kirsty Wark

Politics: Poli, a Latin word meaning 'many'; and tics, meaning 'bloodsucking creatures'.

Robin Williams

The healthy stomach is nothing if not conservative. Few radicals have good digestions.

Samuel Butler

A politician needs the ability to foretell what is going to happen tomorrow, next week, next month and next year. And to have the ability afterwards to explain why it didn't happen.

Winston Churchill

I would rather be an opportunist and float than go to the bottom with my principles round my neck.

Stanley Baldwin

Politics is the art of the possible.

Otto von Bismarck

Politics is not the art of the possible. It consists in choosing between the disastrous and the unpalatable.

J.K. Galbraith

Politics is the art of preventing people from taking part in affairs which properly concern them.

Paul Valéry

Politics is the art of looking for trouble, finding it whether it exists or not, diagnosing it incorrectly, and applying the wrong remedy.

Ernest Benn

Politics has always been the systematic organisation of hatreds.

Henry Brooks Adams

The art of politics consists in knowing precisely when it is necessary to hit an opponent slightly below the belt.

Konrad Adenauer

Politicians are the same all over. They promise to build a bridge even where there is no river.

Nikita Khrushchev

In politics, a lie unanswered becomes truth within 24 hours.

Willie Brown

Ninety per cent of the politicians give the other ten per cent a bad reputation.

Henry Kissinger

Since a politician never believes what he says, he is quite surprised to be taken at his word.

Charles de Gaulle

Funniest
political **bloopers**

Spare a thought for politicians. When we put foot in mouth, it is soon forgotten. For our leaders, their entanglements in thought and word are recorded for posterity, giving us priceless quotes that may be neither wise nor witty but are inadvertently hilarious.

The report speaks for itself. It's a very good report. It's a very long report. I haven't read the report.
Keith Vaz

You teach a child to read, and he or her will be able to pass a literacy test.
George W. Bush

What a waste it is to lose one's mind – or not to have a mind. How true that is.
Dan Quayle

Italy is now a great country to invest in ... today we have fewer communists and those who are still there deny having been one. Another reason to invest in Italy is that we have beautiful secretaries ... superb girls.
Silvio Berlusconi

It's great to be back on terra cotta.
John Prescott

There are only two types of chancellor: those who fail, and those who get out just in time.
Gordon Brown

Unfortunately, the people of Lousiana are not racists.
Dan Quayle

It's a scandal that there are two and a half homeless people in America.
Michael Dukakis

Trees cause more pollution than cars.
Ronald Reagan

Now is not the time for sound-bites. I can feel the hand of history on my shoulder.
Tony Blair

Death has a tendency to encourage a depressing view of war.
Donald Rumsfeld

I think the voters misunderestimate me.
George W. Bush

I know the human being and fish can co-exist peacefully.
George W. Bush

The objectives remain the same and indeed that has been made clear by the Prime Minister in a speech yesterday that the objectives are clear and the one about the removal of the Taliban is not something we have as a clear objective to implement but it is possible a consequence that will flow from the Taliban clearly giving protection to Bin Laden and the UN resolution made it absolutely clear that anyone that finds them in that position declares themselves an enemy and that clearly is a matter for these objectives.
John Prescott

Our enemies are innovative and resourceful, and so are we. They never stop thinking about new ways to harm our country and our people, and neither do we.
George W. Bush

Let me be clear. Israel is a strong friend of Israel's.
Barack Obama

My fellow Americans, I've signed legislation that will outlaw Russia forever. We begin bombing in 5 minutes.
Ronald Reagan

For seven and a half years I've worked alongside President Reagan. We've had triumphs. Made some mistakes. We've had some sex … er … setbacks.
George Bush, Snr

I am the Jesus Christ of politics. I am a patient victim, I put up with everyone, I sacrifice myself for everyone.
Silvio Berlusconi

It's the economy, stupid

> If all economists were laid end to end, they would not reach a conclusion.
>
> **George Bernard Shaw**

Every economy is uncertain. Referring to this or any economy as uncertain is an unnecessary and pessimistic redundancy.

Bo Bennett

It has been said that arguing against globalisation is like arguing against the laws of gravity.

Kofi Annan

Everyone is always in favour of general economy and particular expenditure.

Anthony Eden

Balancing the budget is like going to heaven. Everybody wants to do it, but nobody wants to do what you have to do to get there.

Phil Gramm

A study of economics usually reveals that the best time to buy anything is last year.

Marty Allen

It's the economy, stupid.

Bill Clinton

There are three kinds of economists: those who can count and those who can't.

Eddie George

If you owe the bank $100, that's your problem. If you owe the bank $100 million, that's the bank's problem.

J. Paul Getty

I hate banks. They do nothing positive for anybody except take care of themselves. They're first in with their fees and first out when there's trouble.

Earl Warren

Economic forecasters were invented to make weather forecasters look good.

Irwin Stelzer

The worse the economy, the better the economists.

Alfred Zauberman

An economist is someone who can't see something working in practice without asking whether it would work in theory.

Walter Wolfgang Heller

Expenditure rises to meet income.

C. Northcote Parkinson

If stock market experts were so expert, they would be buying stock, not selling advice.

Norman R. Augustine

That which costs little is less valued.

Miguel de Cervantes

Growth for the sake of growth is the ideology of the cancer cell.

Edward Abbey

Economics is extremely useful as a form of employment for economists.

J.K. Galbraith

An economist is a man who states the obvious in terms of the incomprehensible.

Alfred A. Knopf

There's no such thing as a free lunch.

Anon

A man can be forgiven a lot if he can quote Shakespeare in an economic crisis.

Prince Philip, Duke of Edinburgh

I'm spending a year dead for tax reasons.
Douglas Adams

It's clearly a budget. It's got a lot of numbers in it.

George W. Bush

Law and order

If this is justice, I am a banana.

Ian Hislop

The law isn't justice. It's a very imperfect mechanism. If you press exactly the right buttons and are also lucky, justice may show up in the answer. A mechanism is all the law was ever intended to be.

Raymond Chandler

I have come to regard the law courts not as cathedrals but casinos.

Richard Ingrams

Lawyer: one skilled in circumvention of the law.

Ambrose Bierce

A jury consists of 12 persons chosen to decide who has the better lawyer.

Robert Maxwell

I am free, no matter what rules surround me. If I find them tolerable, I tolerate them; if I find them too obnoxious, I break them. I am free because I know that I alone am morally responsible for everything I do.

Robert A. Heinlein

I know no method to secure the repeal of bad or obnoxious laws so effective as their stringent execution.

Ulysses S. Grant

The law must be stable, but it must not stand still.

Roscoe Pound

Anger is just and love is just but justice is not just.

D.H. Lawrence

However harmless a thing is, if the law forbids it most people will think it wrong.

W. Somerset Maugham

Any fool can make a rule, and any fool will mind it.

Henry David Thoreau

The law, in its majestic equality, forbids the rich, as well as the poor, to sleep under bridges, to beg in the streets and to steal bread.

Anatole France

Bad laws are the worst sort of tyranny.

Edmund Burke

Loopholes are not always of a fixed dimension. They tend to enlarge as the numbers that pass through wear them away.

Harold Lever

Lawyers, I suppose, were children once.

Charles Lamb

The law was made for one thing alone, for the exploitation of those who don't understand it, or are prevented by naked misery from obeying it.

Bertolt Brecht

You cannot stop the spread of an idea by passing a law against it.

Harry S Truman

Laws are like cobwebs, which may catch small flies, but let wasps and hornets break through.

Jonathan Swift

Laws were made to be broken.

Christopher North

If you have 10,000 regulations you destroy all respect for the law.

Winston Churchill

When you go into court you are putting your fate into the hands of 12 people who weren't smart enough to get out of jury duty.

Norm Crosby

The first thing we do, let's kill all lawyers.

William Shakespeare

Laws are like sausages. It's better not to see them being made.
Otto von Bismarck

Injustice anywhere is a threat to justice everywhere.

Martin Luther King, Jnr

Argument and debate

I am not arguing with you – I am telling you.

James McNeill Whistler

The opposite of a correct statement is a false statement. But the opposite of a profound truth may well be another profound truth.

Niels Bohr

Fight for your opinions, but do not believe that they contain the whole truth, or the only truth.

Charles A. Dana

Those who agree with us may not be right, but we admire their astuteness.

Cullen Hightower

It is by universal misunderstanding that all agree. For if, by ill luck, people understood each other, they would never agree.

Charles Baudelaire

The best way to convince a fool that he is wrong is to let him have his own way.

Josh Billings

I have never in my life learned anything from any man who agreed with me.

Dudley Field Malone

A fanatic is one who can't change his mind and won't change the subject.

Winston Churchill

It's a rare person who wants to hear what he doesn't want to hear.

Dick Cavett

A good listener tries to understand thoroughly what the other person is saying. In the end he may disagree sharply, but before he disagrees, he wants to know exactly what it is he is disagreeing with.

Kenneth A. Wells

It is better to debate a question without settling it than to settle a question without debating it.

Joseph Joubert

If you can find something everyone agrees on, it's wrong.

Morris K. Udall

The most important thing in an argument, next to being right, is to leave an escape hatch for your opponent, so that he can gracefully swing over to your side without too much apparent loss of face.

Sydney J. Harris

Every man has a right to his opinion, but no man has a right to be wrong in his facts.

Bernard Baruch

As we must account for every idle word, so we must for every idle silence.

Benjamin Franklin

Do not think of knocking out another person's brains because he differs in opinion from you. It would be as rational to knock yourself on the head because you differ from yourself ten years ago.

Horace Mann

An objection is not a rejection; it is simply a request for more information.

Bo Bennett

I argue very well. Ask any of my remaining friends. I can win an argument on any topic, against any opponent. People know this, and steer clear of me at parties. Often, as a sign of their great respect, they don't even invite me.

Dave Barry

One of the best ways to persuade others is with your ears – by listening to them.

Dean Rusk

I've never had a humble opinion. If you've got an opinion, why be humble about it?

Joan Baez

Most quarrels amplify a misunderstanding.

André Gide

Persuasion is the resource of the feeble; and the feeble can seldom persuade.

Edward Gibbon

To think is to differ.
Clarence Darrow

I'm sorry, if you were right, I'd agree with you.
Robin Williams

It is impossible to defeat an ignorant man in argument.
William G. McAdoo

Power and influence

Power tends to corrupt, and absolute power corrupts absolutely. Great men are always bad men.

Lord Acton

It is said that power corrupts, but actually it's more true that power attracts the corruptible. The sane are usually attracted by other things than power.

David Brin

Being powerful is like being a lady. If you have to tell people you are, you aren't.

Margaret Thatcher

If absolute power corrupts absolutely, does absolute powerlessness make you pure?

Harry Shearer

It is so difficult, if you are made to stand out a bit from the mass, not to assure yourself that it is all due to some special virtue in yourself. All power or money or place therefore brings a kind of corruption almost inevitably.

Sherwood Anderson

In critical moments even the very powerful have need of the weakest.

Aesop

Money is power.

Andrew Jackson

Nearly all men can stand adversity, but if you want to test a man's character, give him power.

Abraham Lincoln

Numerous politicians have seized absolute power and muzzled the press. Never in history has the press seized absolute power and muzzled the politicians.

David Brinkley

Power is poison.

Henry Brooks Adams

Power is not only what you have but what the enemy thinks you have.

Saul Alinsky

Influence is like a savings account. The less you use it, the more you've got.

Andrew Young

Authority and power are two different things: power is the force by means of which you can oblige others to obey you. Authority is the right to direct and command, to be listened to or obeyed by others. Authority requests power. Power without authority is tyranny.

Jacques Maritain

Knowledge is power.

Francis Bacon

I have always been fond of the West African proverb: 'Speak softly and carry a big stick; you will go far.'

Theodore Roosevelt

You only have power over people as long as you don't take everything away from them. But when you've robbed a man of everything, he's no longer in your power – he's free again.

Aleksandr Solzhenitsyn

Power is the great aphrodisiac.

Henry Kissinger

You can exert no influence if you are not susceptible to influence.

Carl Jung

Human beings are not influenced by anything to which they are not naturally disposed.

Hesketh Pearson

I love power. But it is as an artist that I love it. I love it as a musician loves his violin, to draw out its sounds and chords and harmonies ...

Napoleon Bonaparte

Power? It's like a Dead Sea fruit. When you achieve it, there is nothing there.

Harold Macmillan

> Power corrupts. Absolute power is kind of neat.
>
> **John Lehman**

Political power grows out of the barrel of a gun.

Mao Zedong

Groucho Marx

THE WISEST FOOL IN TOWN

'Humour' said Julius Henry ('Groucho') Marx, 'is reason gone mad', and there is certainly something unhinged and irrational about many of his jokes. When asked to provide a photograph for identification purposes, he said: 'I don't have a photograph. I'd give you my footprints, but they're upstairs in my socks.'

This, like many of Marx's surreal lines, was ad-libbed: his wit bubbled up, pure and unfiltered, from the bottomless well of his comic mind. But at the same time it was all just an act, forged and polished during a long apprenticeship in New York vaudeville, beginning as early as his teens in the early 1900s. The glasses were a stage prop, the eyebrows and the moustache were painted on, and the ridiculous walk was just a visual gag. Unlike most of the film stars whose ranks he joined in the 1930s, Marx, when not in costume, could pass unnoticed in a crowd.

But there is a certain kind of artfully surreal jest that is instantly and unmistakably recognisable as a Grouchoism: 'One morning I shot an elephant in my pyjamas. How he got into my pyjamas I'll never know …' Woody Allen reveres Groucho Marx, and once wrote that he 'was the best comedian this country ever produced. He is simply unique in the same way that Picasso or Stravinsky are.'

✳

Go, and never darken my towels again.

✳

I don't want to belong to any club that will accept me as a member.

✳

I've had a perfectly wonderful evening. But this wasn't it.

✳

Outside of a dog, a book is man's best friend.
Inside of a dog it's too dark to read.

✳

Time flies like an arrow. Fruit flies like a banana.

✳

Why don't you bore a hole in yourself and let the sap run out?

✳

A child of five would understand this. Send someone
to fetch a child of five.

✳

I could dance with you till the cows come home … but I would
rather dance with the cows till you come home.

✳

Many years ago I chased a woman for almost two years,
only to discover that her tastes were exactly like mine:
we both were crazy about girls.

✳

She got her looks from her father. He's a plastic surgeon.

✳

My mother loved children – she would have given
anything if I'd been one.

✳

You go Uruguay, and I'll go mine.

My country, right or wrong

Patriots always talk of dying for their country but never of killing for their country.

Bertrand Russell

My country, right or wrong; if right, to be kept right; and if wrong, to be set right!

Carl Schurz

'My country, right or wrong', is a thing that no patriot would think of saying except in a desperate case. It is like saying, 'My mother, drunk or sober'.

G.K. Chesterton

You can't be a real country unless you have a beer and an airline. It helps if you have some kind of football team, or some nuclear weapons, but at the very least you need a beer.

Frank Zappa

Patriotism is a lively sense of collective responsibility. Nationalism is a silly cock crowing on its own dunghill.

Richard Aldington

If I had to choose between betraying my country and betraying my friend, I hope I should have the guts to betray my country.

E.M. Forster

The greatest patriotism is to tell your country when it is behaving dishonourably, foolishly, viciously.

Julian Barnes

Nationalism is an infantile disease, the measles of mankind.

Albert Einstein

A nation is a society united by a delusion about its ancestry and a common hatred of its neighbours.

William Inge

Patriotism is the last refuge of the scoundrel.

Samuel Johnson

My lands are where my dead lie buried.

Crazy Horse

When I am abroad, I always make it a rule never to criticise or attack the government of my own country. I make up for lost time when I come home.

Winston Churchill

Patriotism is the conviction that your country is superior to all others because you were born in it.

George Bernard Shaw

I would die for my country but I could never let my country die for me.

Neil Kinnock

Breathes there the man, with soul so dead,
Who never to himself hath said,
This is my own, my native land!

Walter Scott

A patriot must always be ready to defend his country against his government.

Edward Abbey

A people that values its privileges above its principles soon loses both.

Dwight D. Eisenhower

A strong nation, like a strong person, can afford to be gentle, firm, thoughtful and restrained. It can afford to extend a helping hand to others. It's a weak nation, like a weak person, that must behave with bluster and boasting and rashness and other signs of insecurity.

Jimmy Carter

A man's feet should be planted in his country, but his eyes should survey the world.

George Santayana

Never was patriot yet, but was a fool.

John Dryden

Ask not what you can do for your country, for they are liable to tell you.

Jack Handey

I showed my appreciation of my native land in the usual way by getting out of it as soon as I possibly could.

George Bernard Shaw

Ask not what your country can do for you; ask what you can do for your country.

John F. Kennedy

Your country needs you.

Lord Kitchener

Britain and the British

Never ask a man if he's from Yorkshire. If he is, he'll already have told you. If he isn't, why embarrass him?

Roy Hattersley

Many people do take pride in being English, but the idea of discussing English nationalism is, in polite circles, rather like talking about an embarrassing itch.

Gavin Esler

Always remember that you are an Englishman and therefore have drawn first prize in the lottery of life.

Cecil Rhodes

I am terribly blunt, having been raised in the English tradition which permits a gentleman to be almost infinitely rude, provided he keeps his voice down.

Raymond Chandler

Continental people have sex lives; the English have hot-water bottles.

George Mikes

It's no longer true that continental people have sex lives whereas the English have hot-water bottles – the English now have electric blankets.

George Mikes

Boasting about modesty is typical of the English.

George Bernard Shaw

Even crushed against his brother in the Tube, the average Englishman pretends desperately that he is alone.

Germaine Greer

An Englishman's mind works best when it's almost too late.

Lord D'Abernon

The American dream is that any citizen can rise to the highest office in the land. The British dream is that the Queen drops in for tea.

Michael Bywater

The real tragedy of England, as I see it, is the tragedy of ugliness. The country is so lovely: the man-made England is so vile.

D.H. Lawrence

It is never difficult to distinguish between a Scotsman with a grievance and a ray of sunshine.

P.G. Wodehouse

The average Englishman does not see why a stranger should accost him with jocosity – many Englishmen do not see why a stranger should accost them at all.

William Lyon Phelps

Wales is a country where Sunday starts early, and lasts several years.

Peg Bracken

For me, England is the most exotic place in the world: the British manners, the stratification of society. You see it even in people's shoes.

Henri Cartier-Bresson

England's not a bad country. It's just a mean, cold, ugly, divided, tired, clapped-out, post-imperial, post-industrial slag-heap covered in polysterene hamburger cartons.

Margaret Drabble

One of the reasons Britain is such a steady and gracious place is the calming influence of the football results and shipping forecasts.

Bill Bryson

The British nation is unique in this respect. They are the only people who like to be told how bad things are, who like to be told the worst.

Winston Churchill

Britain will be honoured by historians more for the way she disposed of an empire than for the way in which she acquired it.

Lord Harlech

An Englishman's mind works best when it is almost too late.

Lord D'Abernon

Britain: the land of embarrassment and breakfast.
Julian Barnes

A soggy little island huffing and puffing to keep up with Western Europe.

John Updike

Europe and the Europeans

> To understand Europe, you have to be a genius – or French.
>
> **Madeleine Albright**

If you are lucky enough to have lived in Paris as a young man, then wherever you go for the rest of your life it stays with you, for Paris is a movable feast.

Ernest Hemingway

Venice is like eating an entire box of chocolate liqueurs in one go.

Truman Capote

Belgium has only one real claim to fame. Thanks to all the wars that have been fought on its soil, there are more dead people there than anywhere else in the world. So, while there's no quality of life in Belgium, there's a simply wonderful quality of death.

Jeremy Clarkson

In the 18th and 19th centuries you weren't considered cultured unless you made the European tour, and so it should be.

Edward Heath

Russia cannot be understood with the mind alone ... Russia has to be believed in.

Fyodor Tyutchev

Europeans and Americans are like men and women: they understand each other worse, and it matters less, than either of them suppose.

Randall Jarrell

Belgium is a country invented by the British to annoy the French.

Charles de Gaulle

I don't like Norwegians at all. The sun never sets, the bar never opens, and the whole country smells of kippers.

Evelyn Waugh

Russia is a riddle wrapped in a mystery inside an enigma.

Winston Churchill

Ireland is a small but insuppressible island half an hour nearer the sunset than Great Britain.

Thomas Kettle

In France, they study men; in Germany, books.

Madame de Staël

In Italy for 30 years under the Borgias, they had warfare, terror, murder, bloodshed; they produced Michelangelo, Leonardo da Vinci and the Renaissance. In Switzerland, they had brotherly love, 500 years of democracy and peace and what did they produce? The cuckoo clock.

Orson Welles

The Americans have called the French 'cheese-eating surrender monkeys', a description I totally disagree with. They left out, 'wine-guzzling'.

William Hague

I don't like Switzerland: it has produced nothing but theologians and waiters.

Oscar Wilde

I look upon Switzerland as an inferior sort of Scotland.

Sydney Smith

Whoever speaks of Europe is wrong, it is a geographical concept.

Otto von Bismarck

Italians always act without thinking, it's the glory and the downfall of your civilisation. A German plans a month in advance what his bowel movements will be at Easter, and the British plan everything in retrospect, so it always looks as though everything occurred as they intended. The French plan everything whilst appearing to be having a party, and the Spanish ... well, God knows.

Louis de Bernières

Holland lies so low they're only saved by being dammed.

Thomas Hood

France is the only place where you can make love in the afternoon without people hammering on your door.

Barbara Cartland

The Irish are one race of people for whom psychoanalysis is of no use whatsoever.

Sigmund Freud

How can you govern a country which has 246 varieties of cheese?

Charles de Gaulle

Nations of the world

> I have recently been all round the world and formed a very poor opinion of it.
>
> **Thomas Beecham**

Contrary to what the politicians and religious leaders would like us to believe, the world won't be made safer by creating barriers between people.

Michael Palin

Immigration is the sincerest form of flattery.

Jack Paar

America is the only country where a significant proportion of the population believes that professional wrestling is real, but the moon landing was faked.

David Letterman

Canada is not really a place where you are encouraged to have large spiritual adventures.

Robertson Davies

America is a vast conspiracy to make you happy.

John Updike

Nothing in India is identifiable, the mere asking of a question causes it to disappear or to emerge as something else.

E.M. Forster

China is a civilisation pretending to be a nation.

Michael Ledeen

Poor Mexico, so far from God and so close to the United States.

Porfirio Diaz

Australia is a huge rest home, where no unwelcome news is ever wafted on to the pages of the worst newspapers in the world.

Germaine Greer

Africa always brings something new.

Pliny the Elder

I dream of the realisation of the unity of Africa, whereby its leaders combine in their efforts to solve the problems of this continent. I dream of our vast deserts, of our forests, of all our great wildernesses.

Nelson Mandela

Of course, America had often been discovered before Columbus, but it had always been hushed up.

Oscar Wilde

America: it's like Britain, only with buttons.

Ringo Starr

Americans are benevolently ignorant about Canada, while Canadians are malevolently well informed about the United States.

J. Bartlett Brebner

When the white missionaries came to Africa, they had the Bible, and we had the land. They said, 'Let us pray'. We closed our eyes. When we opened them we had the Bible and they had the land.

Desmond Tutu

Yes, America is gigantic, but a gigantic mistake.

Sigmund Freud

I find it hard to offer an opinion on New Zealand because when I was there it seemed to be shut.

Clement Freud

Brazil – where the nuts come from.

Brandon Thomas

In fact, the whole of Japan is a pure invention. There is no such country, there are no such people. The Japanese people are simply a mode of style, an exquisite fancy of art.

Oscar Wilde

England and America are two countries separated by a common language.

George Bernard Shaw

Why do I continue to live in America? Why do men go to zoos?

H.L. Mencken

Australians are just British people who are happy.
Craig Hill

Canada is all right really, though not for the whole weekend.
Saki

Winston Churchill

THE GREAT BRITISH BULLDOG

Winston Churchill is one of the few politicians to have written a really good book, and the only world leader to have won a Nobel Prize for literature. He was a historian who had a poet's ear for a resonant turn of phrase, and he was a first-class public speaker, although hampered by a lisp and severe nerves that were overcome only through meticulous preparation.

Churchill's gift for words found its fullest expression after he was called in 1940 to lead Britain in the struggle against Nazi Germany. He succeeded in turning the English language into a weapon of war. His rousing speeches, replete with Shakespearean calls to arms, both expressed the British people's determination to fight Nazism and inspired them to ever more heroic efforts. 'They had the lion's heart,' he later wrote. 'I had the luck to be called upon to give the roar.'

But Churchill was more than a political orator; he was also a fine wit. His barbed ripostes to Lady Astor are legendary – both because they are well known and because they may be invented stories, part of the Churchill myth. But some of them have the authentic Churchillian ring to them. When Lady Astor confronted him with the words 'Sir, if you were my husband, I'd poison your tea', he is said to have replied: 'Madam, if you were my wife, I'd drink it.'

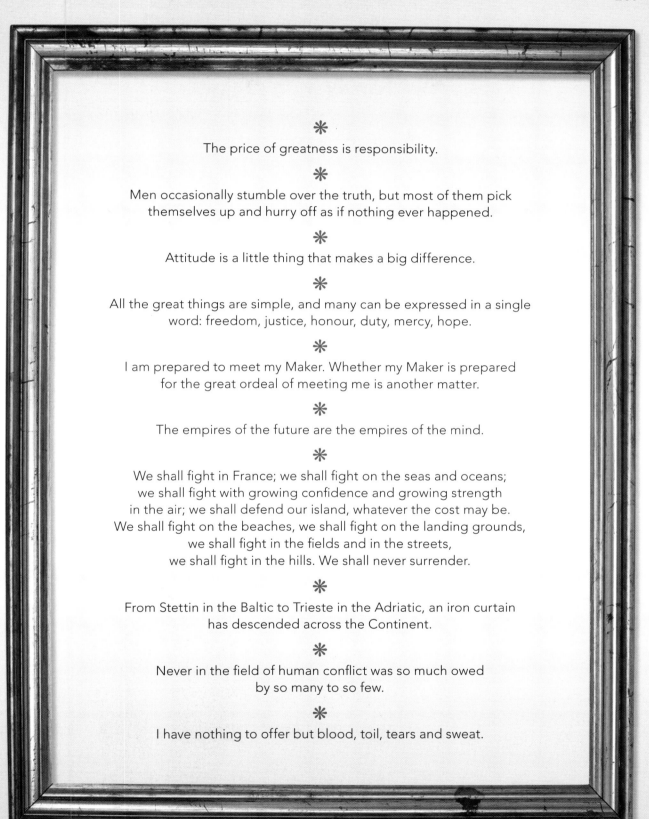

✳

The price of greatness is responsibility.

✳

Men occasionally stumble over the truth, but most of them pick
themselves up and hurry off as if nothing ever happened.

✳

Attitude is a little thing that makes a big difference.

✳

All the great things are simple, and many can be expressed in a single
word: freedom, justice, honour, duty, mercy, hope.

✳

I am prepared to meet my Maker. Whether my Maker is prepared
for the great ordeal of meeting me is another matter.

✳

The empires of the future are the empires of the mind.

✳

We shall fight in France; we shall fight on the seas and oceans;
we shall fight with growing confidence and growing strength
in the air; we shall defend our island, whatever the cost may be.
We shall fight on the beaches, we shall fight on the landing grounds,
we shall fight in the fields and in the streets,
we shall fight in the hills. We shall never surrender.

✳

From Stettin in the Baltic to Trieste in the Adriatic, an iron curtain
has descended across the Continent.

✳

Never in the field of human conflict was so much owed
by so many to so few.

✳

I have nothing to offer but blood, toil, tears and sweat.

Give me liberty

Liberty for wolves is death to the lambs.

Isaiah Berlin

To be free is not merely to cast off one's chains, but to live in a way that respects and enhances the freedom of others.

Nelson Mandela

The only real prison is fear, and the only real freedom is freedom from fear.

Aung San Suu Kyi

If society fits you comfortably enough, you call it freedom.

Robert Frost

I know not what course others may take. But as for me, give me liberty, or give me death.

Patrick Henry

The condition upon which God hath given liberty to man is eternal vigilance; which condition if he break, servitude is at once the consequence.

John Philpot Curran

Freedom is nothing but a chance to be better.

Albert Camus

The moment the slave resolves that he will no longer be a slave, his fetters fall. He frees himself, and shows the way to others. Freedom and slavery are mental states.

Mahatma Gandhi

Freedom is the right to be wrong, not the right to do wrong.

John Diefenbaker

Freedom is always and exclusively freedom for the one who thinks differently.

Rosa Luxemburg

My definition of a free society is a society where it is safe to be unpopular.

Adlai E. Stevenson

I think people should be allowed to do anything they want. We haven't tried that for a while. Maybe this time it'll work.

George Carlin

The tree of liberty must be refreshed from time to time with the blood of patriots and tyrants. It is its natural manure.

Thomas Jefferson

An oppressed people are authorised whenever they can to rise and break their fetters.

Henry Clay

You can have peace. Or you can have freedom. Don't ever count on having both at once.

Robert A. Heinlein

Despots themselves do not deny that freedom is excellent; only they desire it for themselves alone, and they maintain that everyone else is altogether unworthy of it.

Alexis de Tocqueville

People demand freedom of speech as a compensation for the freedom of thought which they seldom use.

Søren Kierkegaard

Oppression can only survive through silence.

Carmen de Monteflores

Freedom is when one hears the bell at 7 o'clock in the morning and knows it is the milkman and not the Gestapo.

Georges Bidault

Be a lamp unto yourself and seek your own liberation with diligence.

Buddha

The most certain test by which we judge whether a country is really free is the amount of security enjoyed by minorities.

Lord Acton

One should never put on one's best trousers to go out to battle for freedom and truth.

Henrik Ibsen

Let every nation know, whether it wishes us well or ill, that we shall pay any price, bear any burden, meet any hardship, support any friend, oppose any foe to assure the survival and the success of liberty.

John F. Kennedy

The right to be heard does not automatically include the right to be taken seriously.

Hubert H. Humphrey

Democracy rules

Democracies don't prepare well for things that have never happened before.

Richard A. Clarke

Democracy is sometimes untidy.

Michael Ancram

The majority of minds are no more to be controlled by strong reason than plumb-pudding is to be grasped by sharp pincers.

George Eliot

It is not worth an intelligent man's time to be in the majority. By definition, there are already enough people to do that.

G.H. Hardy

One-fifth of the people are against everything all of the time.

Robert F. Kennedy

Democracy means simply the bludgeoning of the people by the people for the people.

Oscar Wilde

The more I see of democracy the more I dislike it. It just brings everything down to the mere vulgar level of wages and prices, electric light and water closets, and nothing else.

D.H. Lawrence

Apparently, a democracy is a place where numerous elections are held at great cost without issues and with interchangeable candidates.

Gore Vidal

The great thing about democracy is that it gives every voter a chance to do something stupid.

Art Spander

There is nothing more tyrannical than a strong popular feeling among a democratic people.

Anthony Trollope

Democracy is the name we give the people whenever
we need them.

Robert, Marquis de Flers and Arman de Caillavet

If voting changed anything, they'd abolish it.

Ken Livingstone

Any party that includes the word democratic
in its name isn't.

Patrick Murray

The largest turnout at elections is always where there
is only one candidate.

Peter Ustinov

The ideal form of government is democracy tempered
with assassination.

Voltaire

I am a firm believer in the people. If given the truth,
they can be depended upon to meet any national crises.
The great point is to bring them the real facts.

Abraham Lincoln

Man's capacity for justice makes democracy possible, but
man's inclination to injustice makes democracy necessary.

Reinhold Niebuhr

Democracy is a device that ensures we shall be governed
no better than we deserve.

George Bernard Shaw

Democracy is government by explanation.

A.J. Balfour

It does not require a majority to prevail, but rather an irate,
tireless minority keen to set brush fires in people's minds.

Samuel Adams

Democracy means government by discussion, but it is only
effective if you can stop people talking.

Clement Attlee

It's not the voting that's democracy, it's the counting.

Tom Stoppard

One day the don't-knows will get in, and then where will we be?
Spike Milligan

Democracy is the worst form of government except for all the others that have been tried.

Winston Churchill

War and battle

> In war, truth is the first casualty.
>
> **Aeschylus**

The worst aspect of a war is not the danger of wounds and death from the enemy, but the submission of one's body and soul to brutes and fools in authority.

Martin Boyd

War does not determine who is right only who is left.

Bertrand Russell

In any war, the first casualty is common sense, and the second is free and open discussion.

James Reston

I am not opposed to all wars. I'm opposed to dumb wars.

Barack Obama

The enemy is anybody who's going to get you killed, no matter which side he's on.

Joseph Heller

The quickest way of ending a war is to lose it.

George Orwell

Better to die on your feet than live on your knees.

Emiliano Zapata

A soldier will fight long and hard for a bit of coloured ribbon.

Napoleon Bonaparte

The object of war is not to die for your country but to make the other bastard die for his.

George S. Patton

In war, resolution; in defeat, defiance; in victory, magnanimity; in peace, goodwill.

Winston Churchill

I know not with what weapons World War Three will
be fought, but World War Four will be fought with sticks
and stones.

Albert Einstein

What passing-bells for those who die as cattle?
Only the monstrous anger of the guns …

Wilfred Owen

Better a bad peace than a good war.

Russian proverb

The direct use of force is such a poor solution to any
problem, it is generally employed only by small children
and large nations.

David Friedman

Yes, we love peace, but we are not willing to take
wounds for it, as we are for war.

John Andrew Holmes

War may sometimes be a necessary evil. But no matter
how necessary, it is always an evil, never a good. We
will not learn how to live together in peace by killing
each other's children.

Jimmy Carter

War makes rattling good history; but Peace is poor reading.

Thomas Hardy

War is a most uneconomical, foolish, poor arrangement,
a bloody enrichment of that soil which bears the sweet
flower of peace

M.E.W. Sherwood

It is far easier to make war than to make peace.

Georges Clemenceau

Even war is preferable
to a shameful peace.
Tacitus

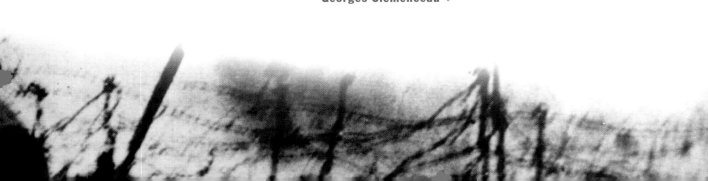

Peace in our time

Peace is not a relationship of nations. It is a condition of mind brought about by a serenity of soul. Peace is not merely the absence of war. It is also a state of mind. Lasting peace can come only to peaceful people.

Jawaharlal Nehru

The object of government in peace and in war is not the glory of rulers or of races, but the happiness of the common man.

William Beveridge

Peace is the only battle worth waging.

Albert Camus

Blessed are the peacemakers: for they shall be called the children of God.

The Bible (Gospel of Matthew)

If we have no peace, it is because we have forgotten that we belong to each other.

Mother Teresa

Since wars begin in the minds of men, it is in the minds of men that the defences of peace must be constructed.

UNESCO Constitution

The right things to do are those that keep our violence in abeyance; the wrong things are those that bring it to the fore.

Robert J. Sawyer

Better than a thousand hollow words is one word that brings peace.

Buddha

Enough of blood and tears. Enough.

Yitzhak Rabin

It's possible to disagree with someone about the ethics of non-violence without wanting to kick his face in.

Christopher Hampton

You can't switch on peace like a light.

Mo Mowlam

The world will never have lasting peace so long as men reserve for war the finest human qualities. Peace, no less than war, requires idealism and self-sacrifice and a righteous and dynamic faith.

John Foster Dulles

If you want to make peace, you don't talk to your friends. You talk to your enemies.

Moshe Dayan

To live without killing is a thought which could electrify the world, if men were only capable of staying awake long enough to let the idea soak in.

Henry Miller

If you want peace, you must work for justice.

Pope Paul VI

I have no secret methods. I know no diplomacy save that of truth. I have no weapon but non-violence. I may be unconsciously led astray for a while, but not for all time.

Mahatma Gandhi

People sleep peaceably in their beds at night only because rough men stand ready to do violence on their behalf.

George Orwell

To reach peace, teach peace.

Pope John Paul II

They shall beat their swords into plowshares, and their spears into pruning-hooks: nation shall not lift up sword against nation, neither shall they learn war any more.

The Bible (Isaiah)

Those who love peace must learn to organise as well as those who love war.

Martin Luther King, Jnr

Peace is always beautiful.

Walt Whitman

You can't separate peace from freedom because no one can be at peace unless he has his freedom.

Malcolm X

History teaches us

God cannot alter the past; only historians do that.
Simon Jenkins

History teaches us that men and nations behave wisely once they have exhausted all other alternatives.

Abba Eban

What experience and history teach is this – that people and governments have never learned anything from the study of history, or acted on principles deduced from it.

G.W.F. Hegel

One of the lessons of history is that nothing is often a good thing to do and always a clever thing to say.

Will Durant

History is a vast early warning system.

Norman Cousins

In times like these, it helps to recall that there have always been times like these.

Paul Harvey

History will be kind to me for I intend to write it.

Winston Churchill

Human history becomes more and more a race between education and catastrophe.

H.G. Wells

History is much decried; it is a tissue of errors, we are told no doubt correctly; and rival historians expose each other's blunders with gratification. Yet the worst historian has a clearer view of the period he studies than the best of us can hope to form of that in which we live.

Robert Louis Stevenson

History is too important to be left to historians.

Robert Harris

History does not always repeat itself. Sometimes it just yells 'Can't you remember anything I told you?' and lets fly with a club.

John W. Campbell

The great nations have always acted like gangsters, and the small nations like prostitutes.

Stanley Kubrick

History is a pack of lies about events that never happened told by people who weren't there.

George Santayana

History is an endless repetition of the wrong way of living.

Lawrence Durrell

The world is full of people whose notion of a satisfactory future is, in fact, a return to the idealised past.

Robertson Davies

History is but glorification of murderers and robbers.

Karl Popper

History repeats itself. That's one of the things wrong with history.

Clarence Darrow

History repeats itself. Historians repeat each other.

Philip Guedalla

History is the sound of hobnailed boots ascending the staircase and of silk slippers coming down.

Voltaire

Historians are like deaf people who go on answering questions that no one has asked them.

Leo Tolstoy

In every age 'the good old days' were a myth. No one ever thought they were good at the time. For every age has consisted of crises that seemed intolerable to the people who lived through them.

Brooks Atkinson

History is more or less bunk.

Henry Ford

> The past is the only dead thing that smells sweet.
>
> **Edward Thomas**

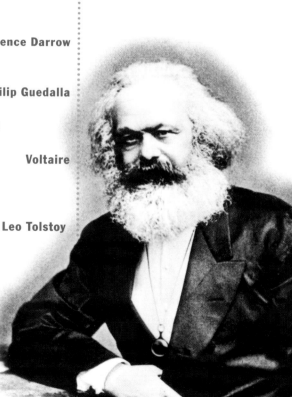

History repeats itself – first as tragedy, then as farce.

Karl Marx

KARL MARX

SIGMUND FREUD

MOTHER TERESA

RICHARD BRANSON

F. SCOTT FITZGERALD

ERNEST HEMINGWAY

P.G

CHARLES DE GAULLE

W. SOMERSET MAUGHAM

PETER USTINOV

MICHELANGELO

EDDIE IZZARD

ALBERT CAMUS

ALAN BENNETT

GEORGE BERNARD

JOAN RIVERS

JONATHAN SWIFT

QUENTIN CRISP

W.H. AUDEN

MUHAMMAD ALI

DOLLY PARTON

JEAN-PAUL SARTRE

GEORGE ORWELL

WALT DISNEY

DOUGLAS ADAMS

JOHN F. KENNEDY

DOROTHY PARKER

ALBERT EINSTEIN

NELSON MANDELA

FRANK ZAPPA

OSCAR WILDE

MARGARET THATCHER

PABLO PICASSO AESOP MARK TWAIN

LEO TOLSTOY

ORSON WELLES ISAAC ASIMOV

VODEHOUSE BILL CLINTON BUDDHA GROUCHO MARX

VIRGINIA WOOLF

JANE AUSTEN SAMUEL PEPYS

W.C. FIELDS MARILYN MONROE

SHAW MAE WEST

BERTRAND RUSSELL

NAPOLEON BONAPARTE

THE WORLD AROUND US

The body and the senses

What is man, when you come to think upon him, but a minutely set, ingenious machine for turning, with infinite artfulness, the red wine of Shiraz into urine.

Isak Dinesen

I have everything now that I had 20 years ago – except now it's all lower.

Gypsy Rose Lee

It's hard to be naked and not be upstaged by your nipples.

Susan Sarandon

Imprisoned in every fat man a thin one is wildly signalling to be let out.

Cyril Connolly

My brain? It's my second favourite organ.

Woody Allen

Man could not have attained his present dominant position in the world without the use of his hands, which are so admirably adapted to act in obedience to his will.

Charles Darwin

What they call 'heart' lies much lower than the fourth waistcoat button.

Georg Christoph Lichtenberg

If any thing is sacred the human body is sacred.

Walt Whitman

We live on the leash of our senses.

Diane Ackerman

I wish I loved the Human Race;
I wish I loved its silly face;
I wish I liked the way it walks;
I wish I liked the way it talks;
And when I'm introduced to one,
I wish I thought 'What Jolly Fun!'

Walter Alexander Raleigh

The body is a sacred garment.

Martha Graham

The body is but a pair of pincers set over a bellows and a stewpot, and the whole fixed on stilts.

Samuel Butler

If soul may look and body touch, which is the more blest?

W.B. Yeats

Whatever withdraws us from the power of our senses; whatever makes the past, the distant, or the future predominate over the present, advances us in the dignity of thinking beings.

Samuel Johnson

I want all my senses engaged. Let me absorb the world's variety and uniqueness.

Maya Angelou

What a piece of work is a man! how noble in reason! how infinite in faculties! in form and moving, how express and admirable! in action, how like an angel! in apprehension, how like a god!

William Shakespeare

O for a life of sensations rather than of thoughts!

John Keats

Thy lips are like a thread of scarlet, and thy speech is comely: thy temples are like a piece of a pomegranate within thy locks. Thy neck is like the tower of David builded for an armoury, whereon there hang a thousand bucklers, all shields of mighty men.

The Bible (Song of Solomon)

The function of muscle is to pull and not to push, except in the case of the genitals and the tongue.

Leonardo da Vinci

Our body is a machine for living. It is organised for that, it is its nature. Let life go on in it unhindered and let it defend itself, it will do more than if you paralyse it by encumbering it with remedies.

Leo Tolstoy

He wore his baldness like an expensive hat.

Gloria Swanson

> *I keep on having my hair cut, but it keeps growing again.*
> **G.K. Chesterton**

If I see something sagging, dragging or bagging, I'm going to have the stuff tucked or plucked.

Dolly Parton

The human race

> Man is the only creature that refuses to be what he is.
> **Albert Camus**

Many things there are, weird and wonderful, none more so than man. He sails beyond the seas, lashed white by winter wind, piercing the waters roaring round ... In all things he finds him a way.

Sophocles

All modern men are descended from a worm-like creature, but it shows more on some people.

Will Cuppy

Man is indeed a being apart ... He has not only escaped natural selection himself, but he is actually able to take away some of that power from nature which before his appearance she universally exercised.

Alfred Wallace

We are at the very beginning of time for the human race. It is not unreasonable that we grapple with problems. But there are tens of thousands of years in the future. Our responsibility is to do what we can, learn what we can, improve the solutions, and pass them on.

Richard P. Feynman

Most human beings have an almost infinite capacity for taking things for granted.

Aldous Huxley

Man is a complex being: he makes deserts bloom – and lakes die.

Gil Stern

Man is distinguished from all other creatures by the faculty of laughter.

Joseph Addison

I hope that people will finally come to realise that there is only one 'race' – the human race – and that we are all members of it.

Margaret Atwood

We're a planet of nearly 6 billion ninnies living in a civilisation that was designed by a few thousand amazingly smart deviants.

Scott Adams

Sooner or later every one of us breathes an atom that has been breathed before by anyone you can think of who has lived before us – Michelangelo or George Washington or Moses.

Jacob Bronowski

We ought to think that we are one of the leaves of a tree, and the tree is all humanity. We cannot live without the others, without the tree.

Pablo Casals

Man is an animal which, alone among the animals, refuses to be satisfied by the fulfilment of animal desires.

Alexander Graham Bell

Man is the only animal that laughs and weeps, for he is the only animal that is struck with the difference between what things are and what they ought to be.

William Hazlitt

Man is the only animal that can remain on friendly terms with the victims he intends to eat until he eats them.

Samuel Butler

I would feel more optimistic about a bright future for man if he spent less time proving that he can outwit nature and more time tasting her sweetness and respecting her seniority.

E.B. White

It is of interest to note that while some dolphins are reported to have learned English, up to 50 words used in correct context, no human being has been reported to have learned dolphinese.

Carl Sagan

We all have the extraordinary coded within us, waiting to be released.

Jean Houston

The world is very different now. For man holds in his mortal hands the power to abolish all forms of human poverty, and all forms of human life.

John F. Kennedy

> Man, I can assure you, is a nasty creature.
> **Molière**

> Man is only a reed, the weakest thing in nature; but he is a reed that thinks.
> **Blaise Pascal**

Pithy insults

Don't get on the wrong side of a great wit. The pen or tongue will be sharpened and sweet revenge brought down on the offender's head. There is an art to the well-turned insult, capable of deflating any reputation in just a few words. Beware.

Her virtue was that she said what she thought, her vice that what she thought didn't amount to much.
Peter Ustinov

I didn't attend the funeral, but I sent a nice letter saying that I approved of it.
Mark Twain

Whenever Clare Short wrestles with her conscience, she wins.
Ben Macintyre

He can compress the most words into the smallest ideas of any man I ever met.
Abraham Lincoln

I never forget a face, but in your case I'll be glad to make an exception.
Groucho Marx

No one can have a higher opinion of him than I have, and I think he's a dirty little beast.
W.S. Gilbert

I heard his library burned down and both books were destroyed – and one of them hadn't even been coloured in yet.
Robertson Davies

A waste of skin.
Lancashire expression

You have delighted us long enough.
Jane Austen

Like being savaged by a dead sheep.
Denis Healey (on being criticised by Geoffrey Howe in the House of Commons)

Peter Mandelson has the insolent manner of one born to the top rung but three.
Gore Vidal

I don't like country music, but I don't mean to denigrate those who do. And for the people who like country music, denigrate means put down.
Bob Newhart

Sometimes when you look in his eyes you get the feeling that someone else is driving.
David Letterman

He has all the virtues I dislike and none of the vices I admire.
Winston Churchill

His lack of education is more than compensated for by his keenly developed moral bankruptcy.
Woody Allen

What's on your mind, if you will allow the overstatement?
Fred Allen

He is one of those people who would be enormously improved by death.
Saki

He has all the characteristics of a dog – except loyalty.
Sam Houston

Fine words! I wonder where you stole them.
Jonathan Swift

You must come again when you have less time.
Walter Sickert

Pets and animals

Biologically speaking, if something bites you, it is more likely to be female.
Desmond Morris

Honey bees are amazing creatures. I mean, think about it, do earwigs make chutney?

Eddie Izzard

I watched a herd of elephants travelling through dense forest – pacing along as if they had an appointment with the end of the world.

Isak Dinesen

Animals are such agreeable friends – they ask no questions, they pass no criticisms.

George Eliot

We call them dumb animals, and so they are, for they cannot tell us how they feel, but they do not suffer less because they have no words.

Anna Sewell

The dog is the god of frolic.

Henry Ward Beecher

The greatness of a nation and its moral progress can be judged by the way its animals are treated.

Mahatma Gandhi

Aerodynamically, the bumblebee shouldn't be able to fly, but the bumblebee doesn't know it so it goes on flying anyway.

Mary Kay Ash

You enter into a certain amount of madness when you marry a person with pets.

Nora Ephron

They will listen to your problems and never ask a thing in return. They will be your friends for ever. And when you get tired of them, you can kill and eat them. Perfect.

Bill Bryson

I hate a word like 'pets': it sounds so much like something with no living of its own.

Elizabeth Jennings

I never saw a wild thing sorry for itself.

D.H. Lawrence

To my mind, the only possible pet is a cow. Cows love you. Until one has loved an animal, a part of one's soul remains unawakened.

Anatole France

You can put wings on a pig, but you don't make it an eagle.

Bill Clinton

Don't accept your dog's admiration as conclusive evidence that you are wonderful.

Ann Landers

You can know the name of a bird in all the languages of the world, but when you're finished, you'll know absolutely nothing whatever about the bird. So let's look at the bird and see what it's doing – that's what counts. I learned very early the difference between knowing the name of something and knowing something.

Richard P. Feynman

I like pigs. Dogs look up to us. Cats look down on us. Pigs treat us as equals.

Winston Churchill

There are 350 varieties of shark, not counting loan and pool.

L.M. Boyd

Cats regard people as warm-blooded furniture.

Jacquelyn Mitchard

Authors like cats because they are such quiet, lovable, wise creatures, and cats like authors for the same reasons.

Robertson Davies

There is nothing in which the birds differ more from man than the way in which they can build and yet leave a landscape as it was before.

Robert Lynd

Our perfect companions never have fewer than four feet

Colette

The great outdoors

> I am not the type who wants to go back to the land; I am the type who wants to go back to the hotel.
>
> **Fran Lebowitz**

I never go through the home counties in summer without a resentful feeling that all the trees and fields and the cows in the fields have had their hair combed and brushed every morning.

Stephen Gwynn

I just wish the world was twice as big and half of it was still unexplored.

David Attenborough

Night is a dead monotonous period under a roof; but in the open world it passes lightly, with its stars and dews and perfumes, and the hours are marked by changes in the face of nature.

Robert Louis Stevenson

Our ancestors worshipped the sun, and they were not that foolish. It makes sense to revere the Sun and the stars, for we are their children.

Carl Sagan

Anyone can be good in the country. There are no temptations there.

Oscar Wilde

I am always most religious upon a sunshiny day.

Lord Byron

May your trails be crooked, winding, lonesome, dangerous, leading to the most amazing view. May your mountains rise into and above the clouds.

Edward Abbey

For congenial sympathy, for poetry, for work, for original feeling and expression, for perfect companionship with one's friends – give me the country.

D.H. Lawrence

There is nothing good to be had in the country, or if there is, they will not let you have it.

William Hazlitt

Climb the mountains and get their good tidings. Nature's peace will flow into you as sunshine flows into trees. The winds will blow their own freshness into you, and the storms their energy, while cares will drop away from you like the leaves of autumn.

John Muir

The country is laid out in a haphazard, sloppy fashion, offensive to the organised mind.

Alan Brien

The reason I love the sea I cannot explain – it's physical. When you dive you begin to feel like an angel. It's a liberation of your weight.

Jacques-Yves Cousteau

The summer and the country have no charms for me. I look forward anxiously to the return of bad weather, coal fires, and good society in a crowded city. I have no relish for the country; it is a kind of healthy grave.

Sydney Smith

Nothing is more beautiful than the loveliness of the woods before sunrise.

George Washington Carver

God made the country, and man made the town.

William Cowper

I hate the outdoors. To me the outdoors is where the car is.

Will Durst

I am at two with nature.

Woody Allen

Gardens and flowers

Flowers pledge no allegiance to banners of any man.
Alice Walker

The earth laughs in flowers.

e e cummings

If I had but two loaves of bread, I would sell one and buy hyacinths, for they would feed my soul.

The Quran

A house with daffodils in it is a house lit up, whether or no the sun be shining outside. Daffodils in a green bowl – and let it snow if it will.

A.A. Milne

Flowers are restful to look at. They have neither emotions nor conflicts.

Sigmund Freud

There is no gardening without humility. Nature is constantly sending even its oldest scholars to the bottom of the class for some egregious blunder.

Alfred Austin

One of the healthiest ways to gamble is with a spade and a package of garden seeds.

Dan Bennett

The Amen of nature is always a flower.

Oliver Wendell Holmes

I hope that while so many people are out smelling the flowers, someone is taking the time to plant some.

Herbert Rappaport

Flowers are the sweetest things God ever made and forgot to put a soul into.

Henry Ward Beecher

A garden is half-made when it is well planned. The best gardener is the one who does the most gardening by the winter fire.

Liberty Hyde Bailey

If a man be wearied with overmuch study, there is no better place in the world to recreate himself than a garden, there being no sense but may be delighted therein.

William Coles

God Almighty first planted a garden; and, indeed,
it is the purest of human pleasure.

Francis Bacon

St Francis ordered a plot to be set aside for the cultivation of
flowers when the convent garden was made, in order that all
who saw them might remember the Eternal Sweetness.

Thomas of Celano

My garden is my most beautiful masterpiece.

Claude Monet

All through the days of childhood the garden is our fairy-
ground of sweet enchantment and innocent wonder.

E.V. Boyle

I have nothing against gardening. I just prefer not to
be there when it happens.

Tracey MacLeod

My philistine of a husband often told with amusement
how a cousin when asked when he expected to finish his
garden replied 'Never, I hope.' And that, I think, applies
to all true gardeners.

Margery Fish

And the Lord shall guide thee continually
… thou shalt be like a watered garden.

The Bible (Isaiah)

Who loves a garden, still his Eden keeps.

Amos Bronson Alcott

A garden is a beautiful book, writ by the finger of God.
Every flower and every leaf is a letter.

Douglas Jerrold

I do not envy the owners of very large gardens. The garden
should fit its master or his tastes, just as his clothes do; it
should be neither too large nor too small, but just comfortable.

Gertrude Jekyll

Scents are the souls of flowers: they may even be perceptible
in the land of shadows.

Joseph Joubert

> The fairest thing in
> nature, a flower, still
> has its roots in earth
> and manure.
>
> **D.H. Lawrence**

Plants and trees

In the woods I am blessed. Happy is everyone in the woods. Oh God! What glory in the woodland.

Ludwig van Beethoven

Love thy neighbour, but pull not down thy hedge.

English proverb

The tree which moves some to tears of joy is in the eyes of others only a green thing which stands in the way.

William Blake

The trees that are slow to grow bear the best fruit.

Molière

Below me trees unnumbered rise,
Beautiful in various dyes;
The gloomy pine, the poplar blue,
The yellow beech, the sable yew,
The slender fir that taper grows,
The sturdy oak with broad-spread boughs.

John Dyer

The true meaning of life is to plant trees, under whose shade you do not expect to sit.

Nelson Henderson

I like to tease my plants. I water them with ice cubes.

Steven Wright

All theory is grey, but the golden tree of life grows green.

Johann Wolfgang von Goethe

When I pick a twig of bay, or brush against a bush of rosemary, or tread upon a tuft of thyme, or pass through incense-laden brakes of cistus, I feel that here is all that is best and purest and most refined, and nearest to poetry, in the range of faculty of the sense of smell.

Gertrude Jekyll

Even if I knew that tomorrow the world would go to pieces, I would still plant my apple tree.

Martin Luther King, Jnr

The greatest mystery of this bursting forth of plants is that it is done when the growth is at its tenderest age; when the shoot is tender and brittle it has power to push through everything that binds it down.

Henry Nicholson Ellacombe

Cabbage: A familiar kitchen-garden vegetable about as large and wise as a man's head.

Ambrose Bierce

Solitary trees, if they grow at all, grow strong.

Winston Churchill

Birth, life and death – each took place on the hidden side of a leaf.

Toni Morrison

What was paradise? But a garden and orchard of trees and herbs, full of all pleasure? What can your eyes desire to see, your ears to hear, your mouth to taste, or your nose to smell, that is not to be had in an orchard?

William Lawson

My main ambition as a gardener is to water my orange trees with gin, then all I have to do is squeeze the juice into a glass.

W.C. Fields

I think that I shall never see
A poem lovely as a tree.

Joyce Kilmer

A plant oft removed cannot thrive.

English proverb

A woodland in full colour is awesome as a forest fire, in magnitude at least, but a single tree is like a dancing tongue of flame to warm the heart.

Hal Borland

Woodman, spare that tree!
Touch not a single bough!
In youth it sheltered me,
And I'll protect it now.

George Pope Morris

Of all the wonders of nature, a tree in summer is perhaps the most remarkable; with the possible exception of a moose singing 'Embraceable You' in spats.

Woody Allen

I like trees because they seem more resigned to the way they have to live than other things do.
Willa Cather

The weather and the seasons

Everybody talks about the weather, but nobody does anything about it.

Charles Dudley Warner

Winter is on my head, but eternal spring is in my heart.

Victor Hugo

Live each season as it passes; breathe the air, drink the drink, taste the fruit, and resign yourself to the influences of each.

Henry David Thoreau

In the spring, at the end of the day, you should smell like dirt.

Margaret Atwood

People don't notice whether it's winter or summer when they're happy.

Anton Chekhov

There's something good in all weathers. If it don't happen to be good for my work today, it's good for some other man's.

Charles Dickens

Ah, summer, what power you have to make us suffer and like it.

Russell Baker

Autumn is a second spring when every leaf is a flower.

Albert Camus

There is always in February some one day, at least, when one smells the yet distant, but surely coming summer … and with it the glad certainty that the good things promised will never fail.

Gertrude Jekyll

The lusty spring smells well, but drooping autumn tastes well.

John Webster

There is a muscular energy in sunlight corresponding to the spiritual energy of wind.

Annie Dillard

When all is said and done, the weather and love are the two elements about which one can never be sure.

Alice Hoffman

The thin snow now driving from the north consists of those beautiful star crystals, perfect little wheels with six spokes ... wheels of the storm chariots.

Henry David Thoreau

Winter is an etching, spring a watercolour, summer an oil painting and autumn a mosaic of them all.

Stanley Horowitz

It was one of those perfect English autumnal days which occur more frequently in memory than in life.

P.D. James

Delicious autumn! My very soul is wedded to it, and if I were a bird I would fly about the earth seeking the successive autumns.

George Eliot

The way to ensure summer in England is to have it framed and glazed in a comfortable room.

Horace Walpole

Thanks heavens, the sun has gone in, and I don't have to go out and enjoy it.

Logan Pearsall Smith

Spring is nature's way of saying 'Let's party!'
Robin Williams

Weather forecast for tonight: dark.
George Carlin

A lot of people **like snow.** I find it to be an **unnecessary freezing** of water.

Carl Reiner

Snow is no winding-sheet, none of the covering of death; it is the warm wrapping mantle of beauty asleep.

Francis King

We shall never be content until each man makes his own weather and keeps it to himself.

Jerome K. Jerome

How do the men who drive the snowplough get to work in the morning?

Steven Wright

Albert Einstein

AN UNLIKELY GENIUS

He made his name in physics, but Albert Einstein's fame extends far beyond that challenging realm of study. In his lifetime he was the symbol of scientific brilliance, the archetype of a nutty professor, known for his comical absent-mindedness (he claimed he could not remember his own phone number) and for many professorly eccentricities such as an intense dislike for socks.

Einstein's life was also a kind of fairytale, since he was an intellectual ugly duckling who showed absolutely no promise at school. His early years in Germany left him with a lifelong distrust of formal education, and a modesty about his own gifts that constantly astonished people. In later life, his self-effacing manner and warm humanism helped to make him a kind of secular saint in the eyes of his admirers.

The great theory associated with Einstein, relativity, went almost unnoticed when it was published in 1905. He was at that time a lowly 26-year-old clerk in the Swiss patent office. Though everyone now knows the idea belongs to Einstein, few could say what relativity is – and somehow this adds to Einstein's mystique. The same is true of his most famous quotation, which is not a quip or a *bon mot*, but a mathematical formula, $E = mc2$, that seems to contain the very secret of the universe.

If *A* is a success in life, then *A* equals *x* plus *y* plus *z*. Work is *x*;
y is play; and *z* is keeping your mouth shut.

The important thing is not to stop questioning. Curiosity has its own
reason for existing. One cannot help but be in awe when one
contemplates the mysteries of eternity, of life, of the marvellous
structure of reality. It is enough if one tries merely to comprehend
a little of this mystery every day. Never lose a holy curiosity.

Before God we are all equally wise – and equally foolish.

Do not worry about your difficulties in mathematics.
I can assure you mine are still greater.

The most beautiful thing we can experience is the mysterious.
It is the source of all true art and science.

To punish me for my contempt for authority,
fate made me an authority myself.

He who joyfully marches in rank and file has already earned
my contempt. He has been given a large brain by mistake,
since for him the spinal cord would suffice.

The distinction between past, present and future is only an illusion,
however persistent.

When I was young, I found out that the big toe always ends up
making a hole in a sock. So I stopped wearing socks.

Back to nature

Nature does not hurry, yet everything is accomplished.
Lao-Tzu

Look deep into nature, and then you will understand everything better.

Albert Einstein

I believe in God, only I spell it nature.

Frank Lloyd Wright

Although human subtlety makes a variety of inventions by different means to the same end, it will never devise an invention more beautiful, more simple or more direct than does nature, because in her inventions nothing is lacking, and nothing is superfluous.

Leonardo da Vinci

The wonders of the visible creation are the footprints of the Creator. Himself as yet we cannot see, but we are on the road that leads to vision.

Pope Gregory I

For four-fifths of our history, our planet was populated by pond scum.

J.W. Schopf

Nature provides exceptions to every rule.

Margaret Fuller

The least movement is of importance to all nature. The entire ocean is affected by a pebble.

Blaise Pascal

You will die but the carbon will not; its career does not end with you. It will return to the soil, and there a plant may take it up again in time, sending it once more on a cycle of plant and animal life.

Jacob Bronowski

THE END IS IN SIGHT

If people think that nature is their friend, then they sure don't need an enemy.

Kurt Vonnegut

Against the laws of nature there is no appeal.

Arthur C. Clarke

This is the foundation of all. We are not to imagine or suppose, but to discover, what nature does or may be made to do.

Francis Bacon

The best remedy for those who are afraid, lonely or unhappy is to go outside, somewhere where they can be quiet, alone with the heavens, nature and God. Because only then does one feel that all is as it should be and that God wishes to see people happy, amidst the simple beauty of nature.

Anne Frank

The sun, with all those planets revolving around it and dependent upon it, can still ripen a bunch of grapes as if it had nothing else in the universe to do.

Galileo

A true conservationist is a man who knows that the world is not given by his fathers, but borrowed from his children.

John James Audubon

Study nature, love nature, stay close to nature. It will never fail you.

Frank Lloyd Wright

The jungle is dark but full of diamonds.

Arthur Miller

The richness I achieve comes from nature, the source of my inspiration.

Claude Monet

Over the long haul of life on this planet, it is the ecologists, and not the bookkeepers of business, who are the ultimate accountants.

Stewart Udall

We have probed the earth, excavated it, burned it, ripped things from it, buried things in it ... That does not fit my definition of a good tenant. If we were here on a month-to-month basis, we would have been evicted long ago.

Rose E. Bird

Science and scientists

> A scientist is a person who knows more and more about less and less until he knows everything about nothing.
>
> **John Ziman**

What is a scientist, after all? It is a curious man looking through a keyhole – the keyhole of nature.

Jacques-Yves Cousteau

The scientific mind does not so much provide the right answers as ask the right questions.

Karl Popper

Electricity is really just organised lightning.

George Carlin

Mathematics, rightly viewed, possesses not only truth, but supreme beauty – a beauty cold and austere, like that of sculpture.

Bertrand Russell

A man has $100 and you leave him with $2, that's subtraction.

Mae West

Science without religion is lame, religion without science is blind.

Albert Einstein

Science is the great cleanser of human thinking; it makes impossible any religion but the highest.

B.H. Streeter

A good scientist is a person with original ideas. A good engineer is a person who makes a design that works with as few original ideas as possible. There are no prima donnas in engineering.

Freeman Dyson

Science is facts; just as houses are made of stones, so is science made of facts; but a pile of stones is not a house and a collection of facts is not necessarily science.

Henri Poincaré

Science may be described as the art of systematic over-simplification.

Karl Popper

I am among those who think that science has great beauty. A scientist in his laboratory is not only a technician: he is also a child placed before natural phenomena which impress him like a fairy tale.

Marie Curie

I believe that a scientist looking at non-scientific problems is just as dumb as the next guy.

Richard P. Feynman

Everybody's a mad scientist, and life is their lab.
David Cronenburg

If I have **seen further** it is by standing on the shoulders of giants.

Isaac Newton

There is no science without fancy; and no art without the facts.

Vladimir Nabokov

Science is an edged tool, with which men play like children, and cut their own fingers.

Arthur Eddington

Archaeology is the peeping Tom of the sciences. It is the sandbox of men who care not where they are going; they merely want to know where everyone else has been.

Jim Bishop

Men love to wonder, and that is the seed of our science.
Ralph Waldo Emerson

Give me a lever long enough and a fulcrum on which to place it, and I shall move the world.

Archimedes

Science is nothing but developed perception, interpreted intent, common sense rounded out and minutely articulated.
George Santayana

The purpose of anthropology is to make the world safe for human differences.

Ruth Benedict

Quantum mechanics: the dreams stuff is made of.

Steven Wright

When you are courting a nice girl an hour seems like a second. When you sit on a red-hot cinder a second seems like an hour. That's relativity.

Albert Einstein

Invention and discovery

Discovery is the ability to be puzzled by simple things.
Noam Chomsky

The most exciting phrase to hear in science, the one that heralds new discoveries, is not 'Eureka!' but 'That's funny ...'
Isaac Asimov

The more you find out about the world, the more opportunities there are to laugh at it.

Bill Nye

If an experiment works, something has gone wrong.

Arthur Bloch

Discovery consists in seeing what everybody has seen and thinking what nobody has thought.

Albert Szent-Györgyi

When you make the finding yourself – even if you're the last person on earth to see the light – you'll never forget it.

Carl Sagan

The world is moving so fast these days that the man who says it can't be done is generally interrupted by someone doing it.

Harry Emerson Fosdick

Every great advance in science has issued from a new audacity of imagination.

John Dewey

Research is the process of going up alleys to see if they are blind.

Marston Bates

I do not know what I may appear to the world; but to myself I seem to have been only like a boy, playing on the sea shore, and diverting myself in now and then finding a smoother pebble or a prettier shell than the ordinary, whilst the great ocean of truth lay all undiscovered before me.

Isaac Newton

Anything that won't sell, I don't want to invent. Its sale is proof of utility, and utility is success.

Thomas Alva Edison

An inventor is simply a fellow who doesn't take his education too seriously.

Charles F. Kettering

Millions saw the apple fall, but Newton was the one who asked why.

Bernard Baruch

Leave the beaten track occasionally and dive into the woods. Every time you do so you will be certain to find something that you have never seen before. Follow it up, explore all around it, and before you know it, you will have something worth thinking about to occupy your mind. All really big discoveries are the results of thought.

Alexander Graham Bell

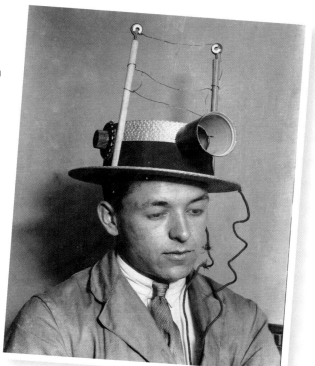

The greatest obstacle to discovery is not ignorance – it is the illusion of knowledge.

Daniel J. Boorstin

The best way to have a good idea is to have lots of ideas.

Linus Pauling

Whenever science makes a discovery, the devil grabs it while the angels are debating the best way to use it.

Alan Valentine

We are trying to understand the fundamental workings of the universe via a language devised for telling one another when the best fruit is.

Terry Pratchett

The best scientist is open to experience and begins with romance – the idea that anything is possible.

Ray Bradbury

Name the greatest of all the inventors. Accident.

Mark Twain

A discovery is said to be an accident meeting a prepared mind.

Albert Szent-Györgyi

The beginning of knowledge is the discovery of something we do not understand.

Frank Herbert

The more original a discovery, the more obvious it seems afterwards.

Arthur Koestler

and outer space

It's very hard to take yourself too seriously when you look at the world from outer space.

Thomas K. Mattingly

It suddenly struck me that that tiny pea, pretty and blue, was the Earth. I put up my thumb and shut one eye, and my thumb blotted out the planet Earth. I didn't feel like a giant. I felt very, very small.

Neil Armstrong

When they discover the centre of the universe, a lot of people will be disappointed to discover they are not it.

Bernard Bailey

Sometimes I think the surest sign that intelligent life exists elsewhere in the universe is that none of it has tried to contact us.

Bill Watterson

God does not play dice with the universe.

Albert Einstein

God not only plays dice, he throws them in the corner where you can't see them.

Stephen Hawking

It may be that the universe is just one of those things that happens from time to time.

Edward Tryon

The universe begins to look more like a great thought than a great machine.

James Jeans

There is no such thing as an empty space or an empty time. There is always something to see, something to hear. In fact, try as we may to make a silence, we cannot.

John Cage

There is a theory which states that if ever for any reason anyone discovers what exactly the universe is for and why it is here it will instantly disappear and be replaced by something even more bizarre and inexplicable. There is another that states that this has already happened.

Douglas Adams

If the universe is expanding, why can't I find a parking space?

Woody Allen

After sleeping through a hundred million centuries we have finally opened our eyes on a sumptuous planet, sparkling with colour, bountiful with life. Within decades we must close our eyes again. Isn't it a noble, an enlightened way of spending our brief time in the sun, to work at understanding the universe and how we have come to wake up in it? This is how I answer when I am asked – as I am surprisingly often – why I bother to get up in the mornings.

Richard Dawkins

There is a coherent plan in the universe, though I don't know what it's a plan for.

Fred Hoyle

The last sound on the worthless Earth will be two human beings trying to launch a homemade spaceship and already quarrelling about where they are going next.

William Faulkner

The more clearly we can focus our attention on the wonders and realities of the universe about us, the less taste we shall have for destruction.

Rachel Carson

We are an impossibility in an impossible universe.

Ray Bradbury

We are just an advanced breed of monkeys on a minor planet of a very average star. But we can understand the universe. That makes us something very special.

Stephen Hawking

Somewhere, something incredible is waiting to be known.

Carl Sagan

There are no passengers on Spaceship Earth. We are all crew.

Marshall McLuhan

Index of names

The publishers have made every effort to find details of all the quote-makers. In some cases this information has proved unobtainable.

Acknowledgments

T = top; B = bottom

COVER All pictures supplied by Rex Features except for pictures of Noël Coward (from Corbis UK Limited), and Groucho Marx and Oscar Wilde (from Getty Images); 4: All pictures supplied by Rex Features except for Robert F. Kennedy, Barack Obama and Spike Milligan (from Getty Images); 11: iStockphoto.com; 12: Getty Images; 15: TopFoto.co.uk; 16: Rex Features Ltd/ITV; 20: iStockphoto.com/Dawn Poland; 21: T iStockphoto.com/Dawn Poland; B iStockphoto.com/Tarek El Sombati; 22: iStockphoto.com/BlackJack3D; 23: T iStockphoto.com/BlackJack3D; B Getty Images; 24: Photo:BMW Group Archives; 27: iStockphoto.com/Tomasz Pietryszek; 28: Rex Features Ltd/Everett Collection; 30: Mary Evans Picture Library; 33: Mary Evans Picture Library; 34-35: iStockphoto.com/Mark Evans; 37: Mary Evans Picture Library/Rue des Archives/PVDE; 40: Getty Images; 43: Mary Evans Picture Library; 44: iStockphoto.com/Keith Webber Jr.; 45: iStockphoto.com/Miiicha; 47: Getty Images; 48: The Kobal Collection/Paramount; 51: iStockphoto.com/Andrzej Tokarski; 52-53: ShutterStock, Inc/Kevin H Knuth; 54: Rex Features Ltd/Richard Young; 56: iStockphoto.com/Kanstantsin Shcharbinski; 57: iStockphoto.com/Kanstantsin Shcharbinski; 59: Getty Images; 61: Mary Evans Picture Library; 62: Mary Evans Picture Library/Classic Stock/H. Armstrong Roberts; 64: ShutterStock, Inc/Johann Helgason; 65: ShutterStock, Inc/Christopher Dodge; 66: Getty Images; 68-69: Corbis/Tomas Rodriguez; 71: Rex Features Ltd/Francesco Guidicini; 73: iStockphoto.com/DNY59; 74: Getty Images/Bill Pierce/Time Life Pictures; 78-79: iStockphoto.com/i-bob; 80: Rex Features Ltd/Matt Baron/BEI; 85: Getty Images; 86: ShutterStock, Inc/Michael D Brown; 87: ShutterStock, Inc/Michael D Brown; 88-89: iStockphoto.com/Mohsen Hafez; 90: ShutterStock, Inc/Alexey Stiop; 93: ShutterStock, Inc/Studio Araminta; 95: Rex Features Ltd; 96: Rex Features Ltd; 98-99: ShutterStock, Inc/Yory Frenklakh; 101: Getty Images/AFP; 102-103: iStockphoto.com/fmatte; 104-105: iStockphoto.com; 106: The Bridgeman Art Library/Private Collection/The Stapleton Collection; 110: ShutterStock, Inc/Atomi; 112: Rex Features Ltd/Francesco Guidicini; 114: Corbis/Bettmann; 117: Rex Features Ltd; 121: Getty Images/Tom Stoddart; 122: The Kobal Collection/Clarence Sinclair Bull; 125: Mary Evans Picture Library; 127: iStockphoto.com/DNY59; 131: Rex Features Ltd/Everett Collection; 132: Rex Features Ltd/Caroline Mardon; 134: iStockphoto.com/Mike Bentley; 135: iStockphoto.com/DNY59; 136: Mary Evans Picture Library/Classic Stock/H.Armstrong Roberts; 138-139: iStockphoto.com/Evrensel Baris Berkant; 140: Getty Images/Hulton Archive; 142: Getty Images; 144: ShutterStock, Inc/James Steidl; 145: iStockphoto.com/ktsimage; 146: Pictorial Press; 147: iStockphoto.com/Red frog;

149: Mary Evans Picture Library; 150: ShutterStock, Inc/J. Helgason; 152-153: iStockphoto.com/Wayne Pillinger; 154: Getty Images; 156: ShutterStock, Inc/cyphix-photo; 157: Getty Images; 158-159: iStockphoto.com/Andrzej Tokarski; 159: ShutterStock, Inc/Terence Mendoza; 162-163: iStockphoto.com/Nikolay Kropachev; 164: TopFoto.co.uk; 167: ShutterStock, Inc/aquatic creature; 168: Rex Features Ltd/Everett Collection; 170: Mary Evans Picture Library/Rue des Archives/PVDE; 172-173: ShutterStock, Inc/BruceParrott; 174-175: Mary Evans Picture Library/Classic Stock/H. Armstrong Roberts; 176-177: iStockphoto.com; 178: iStockphoto.com/Richard Scherzinger; 180: Getty Images; 184: Rex Features Ltd/KPA/Zuma; 186-187: ShutterStock, Inc/Jeanette Qvarfot; 188: Rex Features Ltd/Everett Collection; 191: Getty Images/Jan Persson/Redferns; 192: Reflex Stock/Everett; 194: Rex Features Ltd/CSU Archv; 196: Getty Images; 198: ShutterStock, Inc/Kirill R; 200: The Kobal Collection; 202: Mary Evans Picture Library; 205: Rex Features Ltd/Peter Heimsath; 208: Rex Features Ltd/Steve Bell; 210: ShutterStock, Inc/Vakhrushev Pavel; 212: Rex Features Ltd; 215: Mirrorpix; 218-219: ShutterStock, Inc/Mariano N. Ruiz; 221: The Advertising Archives; 222-223: ShutterStock, Inc/Lou Oates; 225: Rex Features Ltd; 226: Rex Features Ltd/Evening News; 228: Rex Features Ltd/Bill Zygmant; 230: Mary Evans Picture Library; 233: Corbis; 234-235: iStockphoto.com/Christopher Hudson; 236-237: iStockphoto.com/Andrew Johnson; 238: Rex Features Ltd/Dezo Hoffmann; 241: iStockphoto.com/Bernhard Lelle; 244: The Picture Desk/Malmaison Musee du Chateau/Gianni Dagli Orti; 247: Rex Features Ltd/ND; 251: Rex Features Ltd; 252: Mary Evans Picture Library; 254-255: iStockphoto.com/Angela Jones; 256: Corbis/Owen Franken; 258: Getty Images; 261: Mary Evans Picture Library; 262: Getty Images; 264: ShutterStock, Inc/Maximillion69; 266: iStockphoto.com/Hanqauan Chen; 268: Corbis/Bettmann; 271: iStockphoto.com/Nikada; 272: Getty Images; 274-275: Getty Images/Popperfoto; 276-277: iStockphoto.com/Andrey Pustovoy; 279: Getty Images; 282: Rex Features Ltd; 284-285: ShutterStock, Inc/Adisa; 289: ShutterStock, Inc/Dave McAleavy; 290-291: Digitalvision/Joe Cornish; 292: ShutterStock, Inc/Dole; 293: T ShutterStock, Inc/Beata Becla; 294: ShutterStock, Inc/Ewa Walicka; 294-295: ShutterStock, Inc/Elena Elisseeva; 295: ShutterStock, Inc/Elena Elisseeva; 296: Getty Images; 298: Mary Evans Picture Library 2008; 300: Mirrorpix; 302: DK Images; 305: Mary Evans Picture Library; 306-307: ShutterStock, Inc/Eray Haciosmanoglu

THE READER'S DIGEST BIG BOOK OF WIT & WISDOM
is published by The Reader's Digest Association
Limited, 11 Westferry Circus, Canary Wharf,
London E14 4HE.

We are committed both to the quality of our
products and the service we provide to our
customers. We value your comments, so please
do contact us on 08705 113366 or via our
website at www.readersdigest.co.uk

If you have any comments or suggestions
about the content of our books, email us at
gbeditorial@readersdigest.co.uk

Origination by Colour Systems Limited, London
Printed and bound in Europe by Arvato Iberia

Concept code: UK1959/IC
Book code: 400-443 UP0000-1
ISBN: 978 0 276 44557 6
Oracle Code: 250001727S.0024

READER'S DIGEST PROJECT TEAM

Project editor
John Andrews

Art editor
Simon Webb

Designer
Nicola Liddiard

Compiler and writer
Jonathan Bastable

Picture researcher
Rosie Taylor

Indexer
Marie Lorimer

Proofreader
Barry Gage

Research assistants
Aisha Badmus
Sophie Jonathan
Lucinda Newns

Design assistant
Holly Jackman

READER'S DIGEST GENERAL BOOKS

Editorial director
Julian Browne

Art director
Anne-Marie Bulat

Head of book development
Sarah Bloxham

Managing editor
Nina Hathway

Picture resource manager
Christine Hinze

Pre-press account manager
Dean Russell

Product production manager
Claudette Bramble

Senior production controller
Katherine Tibbals